'A thought-provoking book that I, as a professionally qualified youth worker, can use as a tool and a guide to dip in and out of. It's a must-read that is practical, accessible and concise.

The author has provided a complete informative package regarding the use, purposes and needs of forum theatre, highlighting the limitless possibilities of giving those that I work alongside the freedom to engage and express their thoughts and experiences within a safe space and distance with the understanding that there is no right, wrong or judged experience, and with topics and subjects arising through play that are significant to them, and yield realistic solutions, which is vital in youth work.

This book can only be an asset to practitioners and to the individuals and groups they engage with, as it emphasizes the importance of exploration to develop the learning and self-awareness within us all. Both enlightening and powerful.'

Sarah-Jayne Bailey, Qualified Youth Worker, Plymouth

'This book allows the reader to progress from a basic understanding of a forum theatre project to potentially being able to facilitate the project successfully. There is a clear, progressive structure with thorough and detailed examples. It adopts a holistic approach for professionals, and is child-focused, making it a useful tool to support them in managing their social and emotional needs.'

Morven Davey, Head of Inclusion, Ellis Guilford School

'Written for a broad audience by an applied psychologist uniquely placed to apply psychological principles to the therapeutic potential of theatre, this short and very readable book is an excellent source for getting started in this area.

One feels in the safe hands of a practitioner who has walked the talk and shares his experience in a no-nonsense, non-expert but authoritative style.

D1598217

The text can be used as a framework that empowers readers to develop their own approach creatively. Key terms and ideas are explained in a practical way and great care is taken to draw on various forms of evidence that comprehensively illustrate the approach and engage the reader throughout.'

Martin Hughes, Lecturer in Educational Psychology, University of Sheffield

'Nick Hammond's book is a much-needed, stimulating and essential resource for anyone who works with children and young people. It is an inspirational guidebook that gives a nuanced introduction to the dynamics of running forum theatre, and it gives the reader an in-depth appreciation of FT's challenges and creative possibilities. Dr Hammond offers rigorous and empirically grounded insights, alongside vivid case examples to illustrate vital considerations that need to be understood before embarking on a forum theatre project. FT is not for the faint-hearted and this book does an excellent job in showing how it can be used to tackle the difficult task of empowering and listening to those who are disempowered and marginalized. The book demonstrates how psychology and the arts can be used in constructive ways to challenge injustice and oppression; it also shows how to work with children and young people in a collaborative manner to resist oppressive practices and to help them avoid falling into spiralling states of helplessness. This book is highly recommended for educators, community workers, and for all those of us who aspire to give voice to the voiceless, wherever they may be.'

Dr Glenn A. Williams, Senior Lecturer in Psychology, Nottingham Trent University

Forum Theatre for Children

IOEPress Trentham Books

To Cindy, for making it all worthwhile.

Forum Theatre for Children

Enhancing social, emotional
and creative development

Nick Hammond

A Trentham Book
Institute of Education Press

First published in 2015 by the Institute of Education Press, University of London, 20 Bedford Way, London WC1H 0AL

ioepress.co.uk

British Library Cataloguing in Publication Data:
A catalogue record for this publication is available from the British Library

ISBNs
978-1-85856-556-9 (paperback)
978-1-85856-651-1 (PDF eBook)
978-1-85856-652-8 (ePub eBook)
978-1-85856-653-5 (Kindle eBook)

Every effort has been made to trace copyright holders and to obtain their permission for the use of copyright material. The publisher apologizes for any errors or omissions and would be grateful if notified of any corrections that should be incorporated in future reprints or editions of this book.

The opinions expressed in this publication are those of the author and do not necessarily reflect the views of the Institute of Education, University of London.

Typeset by Quadrant Infotech (India) Pvt Ltd
Printed by CPI Group (UK) Ltd, Croydon, CR0 4YY

Cover image ©aquarium graphic design ltd 2014
The illustrations in figure 1.3 are reproduced by kind permission of Cindy Tatum

Contents

List of figures and tables

Glossary of terms

Actor: A child who takes part in forum theatre workshops to devise a play around a given theme. This child will later perform the play with the actor group to spect-actors.

Aesthetic space: A physical space within which the play takes place, such as a classroom, sports hall or park.

Affective dimension: The emotional connection made between spect-actors and the play, including characters. This evokes a reaction from spect-actors that prompts them to attempt change. Associated term: paradoxical theory of change.

Antagonist: The character presenting the challenge to the protagonist. This character may represent a person, system or internal challenge.

Audience: This might include parents, teachers, school governors, representatives from the local authority and so on. Typically the audience comprises observers only, rather than auxiliary facilitators or spect-actors.

Auxiliary facilitator: An assistant to the facilitator. This may be an older or more able peer, teacher or other adult. The role is to support children who might have softer voices or lack the confidence to share their ideas.

Challenge: Originally referred to as oppression by Boal (1979; 1995; 2002). A challenge might be a teacher, a parent, a peer group, a school or care system, or one's own perceptions or anxieties.

Cognition: This refers to a broad range of skills including information-processing, thinking, reasoning and problem-solving. In this book the focus is on *embodied cognition*. This refers to using our bodies to act on our world and, as a result, stimulating all of these cognitive processes.

Condensation: The process of reducing complex ideas into a single idea or action.

Containment: The process of receiving an emotional response from another in a controlled way. To process and acknowledge feelings without becoming overwhelmed. To communicate this understanding back in a calm and measured way.

Counter-transference: The reciprocations of a facilitator toward the child's projected attributions, feelings or thoughts, based on the child's own history. Associated term: transference.

De-role: Games and activities that aim to support children who have been actors in a play to move away from the role and back to reality – that is, from fictional characters to their real selves.

Embodied play: The type of play that makes use of one's own body in the world. Embodied play is an expressive, often overt, form of play. Examples include drama and dance.

Empathy: The ability to see a situation from another person's point of view.

Externalization: The process of placing one's own thoughts, feelings, dreams and so on, into a fictional character and/or story. The process works by making the problem external from oneself. This allows for flexibility to explore the issues in a safe and non-threatening way. Associated term: projection.

Facilitator: The adult who will lead the workshops and later the performance, guiding both actors and spect-actors through the process of forum theatre.

Focus groups: Best described as a group interview. In this book extracts from follow-up discussions were taken from focus groups with actors, spect-actors and teachers.

Forum: The part of the performance where the children get the chance to attempt to make changes to the play in order to reach a more desirable conclusion. This includes swapping roles, hot-seating, discussion and debate.

Hot-seating: A technique used during the workshops and forum where children are asked questions about their thoughts, feelings and motivations, and respond in character.

Huddle: A technique used during the forum to support the actor group in their improvisational response toward spect-actors' suggestions. Led by the facilitator, the aim is to clarify suggestions from the spect-actor, reinforce character motivations, remind actors to keep responses realistic and not to fall into simplistic resolutions, and provide support in response to any questions or concerns they may have.

Key Stage 1: In England and Wales this refers to the period of schooling covering children typically aged between 5 and 7. It includes Year Groups One and Two.

Key Stage 2: In England and Wales this refers to the period of schooling covering children typically aged between 7 and 11. It includes Year Groups Three to Six.

Model: A simple graphical or bullet-pointed outline of the play that replaces a traditional script. For example, a sequence of key events in the play is documented, as opposed to a heavily scripted text.

Paradoxical theory of change: The process whereby a person recognizes their current predicament before being able to make a meaningful change. In forum theatre this is seen in the original play that ends undesirably for the protagonist. Watching the play evokes a strong emotional response that encourages spect-actors to attempt change – initially for the protagonist, with the hope of transferring these solutions to their own lives.

Performance: The collective term to mean both the original play and the forum element in front of spect-actors.

Plasticity: The safety and flexibility of the aesthetic space, which is recognized and felt by spect-actors. The play allows for reality to be suspended, maintaining the distance between the spect-actor and the challenge presented and encouraging the opportunity for change. Associated terms: externalization and aesthetic space.

Play: The original play is created by the actor group in the workshops and presented to spect-actors. A revised play is created when spect-actors offer solutions to help the protagonist overcome their challenge during the forum.

Problem-solving repertoires: The number of possible solutions available to overcome a challenge in real life. These are extended, developed and brought to the child's awareness through the forum theatre process.

Protagonist: The central character facing the challenge from the antagonist.

PSHE: Personal, Social, Health and Economic education forms a flexible part of the curriculum in England. PSHE does not have to be provided as a standalone subject but schools are required to make provision for its inclusion within the curriculum. Due to the non-statutory nature of PSHE there are no standardized criteria regarding what is taught as part of PSHE, when it is taught and how it is taught. The Department for Education in England does provide good-practice guidance, but content is likely to vary greatly between schools. However, models of PSHE and the flexibility provided vary between countries within the United Kingdom.

Rehearsal: An opportunity to try out creative ideas without limitations or fear of failing. Associated term: personal construct psychology, whereby the child is encouraged to rehearse alternative views of the world.

Research community (RC): A community developed through the exploration and discovery of new knowledge around an agreed question or problem. The RC will have shared values, resources and commitment to a project.

Role reversal: The process of swapping roles whereby the child is able to put themselves in the shoes of others. Associated term: person-centred theory, where children can develop insight and empathy.

Social learning theory (SLT): This refers to the potential to learn through observation.

Solutions: During the forum element of the performance, spect-actors suggest and try out new ideas to overcome the presenting challenge. Associated terms: problem-solving repertoires and rehearsal.

Spect-actors: Children in this book who begin their participation at the performance stage. These children watch the original play and then attempt to change its outcome through discussion and role reversal. Spect-actors both observe, as in spectator, and perform, as in actor.

Tableau: Used at the start and end of a scene and when spect-actors shout 'Stop!' Tableau is a freeze-frame made by actors to represent a scene, best likened to a stills picture or pausing a film.

Telemicroscopic: Forum theatre allows for challenges to be magnified. For example, subtleties relating to emotions, actions, words or motivations inherent to the challenge are made more obvious. This allows for greater exploration and more sustainable solutions to be found.

Theme: An overarching idea such as transition, relationships, racism, and so on, which may house smaller, related sub-themes. Sub-themes of transition, for example, might include moving school, moving house or divorce, among others.

Transference: The process whereby the child projects attitudes, feelings, and thoughts from adult figures and experiences in their own histories onto the facilitator.

Warm-up: Games and activities designed to prepare a safe space for children to play through theatre. Preparation includes mental, vocal, physical, sensory and emotional aspects.

Workshops: These allow children the opportunity to develop the necessary skills to devise and perform their own play around a theme. They are completed over a set number of weeks with children from within the setting in which you work.

Vignette: A short one-scene play. Multiples of these can be developed in workshops where there are larger numbers of children.

Extract abbreviations

Extracts from transcripts are used throughout to make and support arguments about forum theatre. Here is a quick reference guide:

AF	auxiliary facilitator
F	facilitator (played by the author)
HT	head teacher of host school
NH	interviewer (author initials)
KS1CT	Key Stage 1 class teacher (typically teaches children aged 5–7)
KS2CT	Key Stage 2 class teacher (typically teaches children aged 7–11)
SA ()	spect-actor who has swapped roles during the forum section. The () with a number may be included to differentiate one spect-actor from the other
SAA	spect-actor discussing or debating from the audience (that is, a spect-actor who has not swapped roles)
Y-SA	'Y' followed by a number (replaced here with a '-') denotes a child belonging to a specific year group who took part as a spect-actor. This code is used for post-FT discussion only
Y6A()	Year Six child who participated in the actor group. The () with a number may be included to differentiate one actor from another

Abbreviations for the Empathy Project only

Y4	a child in Year Group Four.
Y5()	children in Year Group Five. The () with a number may be included to differentiate one actor from another.
Y6	a child in Year Group Six.

There are some additional, but minimal, abbreviations that are explained in the text where applicable.

Author's note

This book contains examples and stories of forum theatre based on two research studies and multiple anecdotes from projects led by the author. All names and identifiable details have been removed to protect anonymity.

Acknowledgements

Books do not create themselves: they are often fronted by an author but supported by a number of people. I would like to take this opportunity to thank those who have offered their support, belief, encouragement and enthusiasm in the creation of this book in one form or another at various points over the years:

Sarah, Jenny, and Bruce Bailey, Deborah Butler, Kim Man Chan, Shinel Chidley, Kathryn Court, Gary Cridland, Smita 'mama' Patel, Vicki Pinches, Leanna Sherren and Cindy, Janet, and Mick Tatum – when it mattered you were there, thank you.

I would like to thank Gillian Klein for her energy, enthusiasm and commitment to this book and extend my gratitude to those who have offered support, commentary, and reflections on this work at various stages: Martin Hughes, Laurie Petch, Michael Pomerantz and Glenn Williams. I would also like to thank everyone at IOE Press for their support throughout the process of creating this book, especially Jonathan Dore and Amanda Dale for their insightful comments and suggestions.

Fusing the arts and sciences is tough in academia and even tougher in practice. I would like to thank Tom Billington, Ruth Illman, Peter Jones, Jackie Lown, Kathryn Pomerantz and Tony Williams for supporting my vision of using the arts within more conventional boundaries. Their contribution to the development of my thinking, and their kindness and support along the way, have been humbly received.

Over the years I have also been supported to no small degree by some incredible arts practitioners and psychologists to whom I am eternally grateful. There are far too many to mention individually, but to those who gave me the space and encouragement to play again and who offered insight, wisdom and apprenticeship through their extraordinary creative endeavours and the practical and funding opportunities they provided – thank you.

To the children and young people I have worked with, thank you for offering no end of inspiration and insight. They teach us all a lesson: if we are prepared to *really listen* to children, we will find that their often remarkable stories are transformative not just for the child, but to adults too. Listening is as much about having an open mind as it is about having open ears – never underestimate how privileged we are to hear children's stories and how important it is for them to be heard. To the head teachers, parents, policymakers and commissioners who have shown confidence and commitment in working with me to run drama projects in their schools, colleges, and other settings – thank you for trusting the process and for your encouraging feedback and support. I would like to extend this acknowledgement to colleagues at the psychology services who supported the research and projects on which this book is based.

Finally, to the children, parents and staff of the school on which a large section of this book is based, who cannot be named for confidentiality reasons. This work is indebted to them; I hope the book serves you well. Thank you to Imogen Newman and Bailey Webster who provided the inspirational ideas for the front cover design and to Shawn Stipling who was able to translate these sophisticated ideas into a wonderful piece of artwork.

About the author

Dr Nick Hammond is an HCPC (Health and Care Professionals Council) registered and a BPS (British Psychological Society) chartered Educational and Child Psychologist, social theatre practitioner and film maker. He is an advocate of empowering and transformative arts and psychology for children, young people and their communities. He has worked extensively in a diverse range of settings as an actor, facilitator, consultant, researcher and psychologist. He has delivered seminars, lectures, and experiential training sessions for students, academics, communities, and professionals across the UK and acted as an external supervisor to postgraduate students on education programmes.

Nick was the founding member of The Arts Lab, a multidisciplinary network of professionals who used the arts in their work. Together with Arts Lab colleagues he co-created the international Arts in Applied Psychology and Education Conference and ran it for five years. His work has focused on empowerment and power distribution, especially in enabling the voice of the child through the dominant adult discourse and political agenda. He has a special interest in the management and resolution of social, emotional and behavioural needs among children and young people.

Listen earnestly to anything your children want to tell you, no matter what. If you don't listen eagerly to the little stuff when they are little, they won't tell you the big stuff when they are big, because to them all of it has always been big stuff.

(Wallace, 2001)

Chapter 1

Setting the scene

It's sort of like you're really helping children to speak up for themselves. 'Cos usually its parents who like say 'ah yeah sure, she's really, really good.'... I never get to really speak up to [them] ... forum theatre sort of helped me, like to get a bit braver, to get to speak up for myself.

(Year Three forum theatre participant. In Hammond, 2013: 8)

Aim of the book

Engaging children as active agents in their own lives is an aim many of us espouse. Whether the task relates to educational or social inclusion, academic achievement, developing effective behaviour systems or emotional skills or making constructive contributions to their community, I believe child-centred practice is not only a legal obligation, but also an ethical and moral one. However, fulfilling this duty can be challenging. Imagine an approach that is flexible enough to engage children in meeting all these duties and that empowers them to take ownership. An approach in which they are autonomous, yet respectful, while learning from each other about issues relevant to their own lives and the wider community. And, as the Year Three (Y3) child above observes, an approach in which they feel liberated by being given a voice so that adults can develop genuinely child-driven policies and practices with them. Welcome to the potential of forum theatre (FT).

This book fuses the art of theatre with the science of psychology. Through practical, evidence-based examples I demonstrate how FT can be used effectively and safely to develop children's social, emotional and creative potential. These accounts aim to be illuminating, encouraging and challenging. However, they are not intended as a recipe for how an FT project should be run. This would inhibit your own creativity and make radical assumptions about your context. My aim is to inspire you to explore, play and try out the ideas and concepts provided to find what's right for your own context. Work *with* children and try to understand what is important to them and their community. This will create an FT experience that feels exciting, contemporary and accessible to your audience.

Not only do I draw together the fields of psychology and theatre – I also contextualize them in the field of education in the broadest sense. Readers may be familiar with FT or it may be new to them. It is likely that most readers will be interested in how children think, behave and feel and how these aspects of their psychology influence what they do; you may already be using approaches informed by psychology, whether or not you are aware of this. I expect readers to include teachers, social workers, youth workers, psychologists, therapists, theatre practitioners, parents and young people and students, among others. The book gives equal consideration to both familiar and unexplored ideas in both theatre and psychology that have practical relevance to working with children. Each stage of the FT process is explored, from workshops to de-role. I hope the book will enable readers to feel encouraged and confident in running and managing an FT project, whatever their level of interest or previous knowledge of psychology or theatre.

How the book is organized

The book focuses on two evidence-based FT projects, supplemented by other illuminative anecdotal examples of FT. Practical examples, theoretical frameworks and original research data illustrate how an FT project is put together. The book is organized according to the sections of a typical FT project within which children develop their own play:

> **Chapter 1** – setting the scene. This chapter introduces FT and explains why and how FT should be used. Context is discussed in relation to the two focus FT projects and followed by a brief introduction to the psychological and theatrical frameworks used in these projects.
>
> **Chapter 2** – the workshops. From warm-ups to creating a dramatic play or vignette, this chapter looks at the function and purpose of the workshop. It explains what is meant by a safe space and how to create one, and discusses how workshops are developed, run and managed. It also shows how children are supported to generate content, character and narrative.
>
> **Chapter 3** – the performance. This chapter explores the two principal components of the FT performance: the presentation of the play and the forum, where the audience attempt to create a more desirable end to the play. Key tools used in the forum are considered: questioning characters in role (hot-seating), encouraging audience members to swap roles (role reversal) and managing discussion and debate. We discover how the original play or vignette can be changed by the spect-actors and how

actors can be supported in improvising their responses, using the 'huddle'. We explore the role of observation, rehearsal, play, problem-solving and finding solutions, and give consideration to the debated role of empathy in FT.

Chapter 4 – de-role and aftercare. FT with children can be perfectly safe and incredibly powerful if the process is effectively managed and planned. This chapter discusses practical games and activities to support de-role and aftercare. De-role is the process of supporting children who have been actors to move away from the play and back to reality and from fictional characters to their real selves. Aftercare refers to planned support for children and adults for issues that may arise from the FT. Safeguarding issues are considered, together with how linking FT to wider community development priorities can support aftercare plans.

Chapter 5 – resources and materials. This chapter provides helpful resources for busy practitioners to help kick-start an FT project.

Chapter 6 – the unanswered questions and research potential of FT. Those studying drama, psychology or education, or professionals who are keen to undertake independent practice-as-research, may be interested in using FT in their own studies. This chapter provides students and others with accessible psychological frameworks, possible research questions and additional practical activities for their own research projects.

A brief introduction to FT: What, who and why?

We will start by introducing the origins of FT, who might use the method and why it should be used.

What?

FT was pioneered by Augusto Boal during the 1970s in South America. Part of a collection of theatrical methods referred to as the Theatre of the Oppressed (Boal, 1979), FT is perhaps the most well-known and widely used of these approaches. FT began as a series of interactive touring plays, referred to as simultaneous dramaturgy (Boal, 1995). Simultaneous dramaturgy involved a group of actors playing to audiences for whom the subject matter of the play personally resonated; these plays would end with a challenge for the central character, the protagonist. Boal would ask the audience for ideas on how the protagonist could overcome the challenge. The actor playing the protagonist would take each idea and improvise a more desirable conclusion to the scene. During one of these plays an audience member began to protest at how her idea was being inaccurately represented by the actor so Boal invited her onto the stage to act out her own solution, and FT was born (Boal, 1995).

There are many variations of FT. Theatre in Education (TiE) companies, for example, may tour a pre-determined play and, like Boal's early incarnation of FT, offer audiences the opportunity to help the protagonist overcome the challenge presented either through suggestion or role-swapping. Others may work with communities to develop a play based on their own challenges, which is then shown to an invited audience that might include parents or teachers. Each variation has its own potential risks and benefits. Whatever variant of FT is used, each project will share a range of common features. Firstly, the FT play is designed to end in an undesirable way for the protagonist due to the actions of an oppressor or oppressors. Boal (1979; 1995; 2002) uses the term 'oppressor' to describe a person, structure or belief system, for instance, that is presenting a challenge to the oppressed. This might be a teacher, a parent, a peer, a school or care system, or the protagonist's own perceptions or anxieties. Thus the oppression in the play can be internal or external, but it is always challenging to the person or collective of people. However, the terms 'oppression' and 'oppressed' are complex and can have very negative connotations, so oppression and oppressor are better referred to as 'challenge' and 'challenger'. We can readily accept that people will experience challenges in their lives, but it can be more difficult to accept that one's actions might be oppressive.

The play is shown to an audience, who in FT terms are known as spect-actors (Boal, 1995; 2002). They first watch the play before being given the opportunity to swap roles with the actors to reach a more desirable conclusion. Thus the audience will be both spectators – hence the use of 'spect' – and later, actors. After the play ends the facilitator – also known as the Joker – will invite the spect-actors to discuss what they have seen. The play is then re-run from the start and the spect-actors are encouraged to shout 'Stop!' as soon as they notice a challenge for the protagonist, and at this point the actors will freeze. The spect-actor who halted the action may then swap roles with an actor, offer suggestions or hot-seat characters with the support of the facilitator. Hot-seating is a process whereby an actor answers questions in character. The process of stopping and starting the play, role-reversal, hot-seating and discussion continues for a set period of time – usually one to two hours. This part of the process, referred to as the 'forum' in this book, can be considered a game: the spect-actor will attempt change whilst the actor playing the antagonist will attempt to remain true to the original model. This helps create a realistic experience for the spect-actors that aims to achieve tangible outcomes and provide a space for discussion about pertinent issues through play.

Who?

Choosing the right facilitator is important. This person – or group of people – will be the link between those who commission the project and the children. The facilitator may be in-house, such as a teacher or teaching assistant or an external agency that already provides services to your setting. Alternatively, the commission might be based on work offered by a TiE company, theatre practitioner or students of applied drama courses. Facilitators have to be right for your setting and the children they will be working with.

Whether you decide to run an FT project independently or commission a project in, there are two questions to consider. First: is the work safe? Second: does the person or group have the qualities you think suitable to run a workshop? (This is especially important if the children are creating the play themselves.) These matters require a little more attention.

Safety is provided by the space that is created mainly by the facilitator. Planning and thoughtful follow-up, closure and de-role activities must be adequate. These points are considered in detail in the book. In addition, it is important that facilitators be mindful of their role in providing containment to the group:

> Containment is thought to occur when one person receives and understands the emotional communication of another without being overwhelmed by it, processes it and then communicates understanding and recognition back to the other person. This process can restore the capacity to think in the other person.
>
> (Douglas, 2007: 33)

This may sound complicated, but many people working with children already offer containment on a daily basis. For example, when a child becomes upset, this may present in a number of ways, such as withdrawing, crying, shouting or even throwing chairs. The adult responds by acknowledging through words and actions that the child is upset and maintains a calm and measured approach, so offering a form of containment. The adult achieves this by communicating back to the child that they have understood the feeling of being upset and that the child is safe. The adult remains composed and able to deal with the upset without exacerbating the situation. This process demands some reflectivity and reflexivity. For example, what does being overwhelmed mean for you? For some this may manifest overtly such as shouting or adopting a closed body language toward the child. For others, being overwhelmed is a covert experience, such as feeling very upset and not processing the experience effectively, thus carrying the negative feelings over until they next see the child.

I am often asked whether FT takes a special person or requires special skills. There are certainly qualities and skills that are important, yet these are not necessarily special. The ideal facilitator will genuinely care about what children have to say; this is a basic prerequisite. But the skill of working with children is more complex, especially when children are developing their own play in FT. The children will create their characters and story based on their own experiences. The facilitator must therefore take time to understand and listen to the children, identifying pertinent themes and checking out these ideas. Listening actively involves being aware of both what is, and what is not, being said, to reflect back and clarify what you have heard or noticed, while not linking the character and story back to the child directly – as discussed later. The facilitator will also listen to adults who support the child, such as parents, carers, friends, teachers, teaching assistants, youth workers and social workers. All these people will add clarity and direction to the work and help identify potential issues that may require follow-up, post-FT. Some of the other skills and qualities the facilitator is likely to have include:

- the ability to work – and enjoy working – with children
- awareness of safeguarding issues and protocols in relation to working with children and young people
- the ability to develop professional rapport with children that is friendly, respectful and fun, while still providing boundaries, leadership and a creative vision to help bring the play together
- the confidence to manage challenging behaviour
- trust in the process of working creatively and valuing play as a genuine way to learn, whatever the age or developmental stage of participants
- the ability to switch confidently between working with children and adults in senior positions and to explain processes in language that is appropriate and accessible to very different audiences
- the ability to co-create a working space with the group, based on shared values
- respect for both the theatrical and the psychological elements inherent in FT projects

- the ability to communicate theatre as a discipline and motivate children toward a shared vision of the final product
- the ability to be mindful, sensitive and non-judgemental
- the ability to trust that children will know what their audience will want and understand from a play.

The focus in this book is on FT developed *with* children, and this list of qualities and skills will optimize the FT process. Many of them are likely to be familiar to those who are already working with children.

Why?

FT offers children the opportunity to explore contemporary issues that are important to them and to find sustainable solutions. Almost any issue can be explored through FT, including bullying, racism, asylum-seeking, unemployment, homelessness, domestic violence, drug awareness, financial management and many more issues relevant to children. FT has been shown to empower children to share their views (Hammond, 2013) and, as this book shows, can help develop children's social, emotional, cognitive and creative potential. Two areas are key in understanding the usefulness of FT: the importance of play and the role of arts in education and politics. They offer a clear rationale for the importance of using FT as a way of working with children and a broader context for the projects presented in this book.

The importance of play

Play is regarded as an innate and important form of human communication, a medium by which children are able to express, create, discover and rediscover themselves and their world. Play is both developmentally important (Delaney, 2010) and essential to the exploration and liberation of one's self (Winnicott, 1971). Delaney suggests that, developmentally, play helps children to learn how to:

- take turns and share
- negotiate and compromise
- work as team players
- accept rules and be socially flexible.

Winnicott argues that play and the closely associated concept of creativity are part of the lifecycle of all human beings and important in maintaining a healthy sense of self. One may assume school-aged children have effectively developed such play skills, but if not, difficulties in social skills are somewhat inevitable. This is especially given the increased demands of the new National Curriculum in England that sees children working at a more sophisticated level than ever before.

As children move through the education system the opportunities to engage in play and arts-based learning are significantly reduced in favour of standardized testing and formalized learning. Yet play and arts remain essential in the learning of important life skills.

THE SOCIO-POLITICAL CONTEXT: ARTS IN EDUCATION AND POLITICS

Context can help guide projects by giving facilitators an understanding of potential opportunities and barriers as well as issues that may need follow-up support. The state of the arts in the British education system and the socio-political issues that may contribute to social exclusion, marginalization, social injustice and disempowerment are key issues that FT aims to challenge.

The Primary National Curriculum in England prescribes drama as a means of increasing the skill of spoken English and classifies it as a largely non-statutory requirement (DfE, 2013a). Yet other art forms, such as music and art and design, retain core subject status. The Secondary National Curriculum is a little more optimistic about the use of drama especially in Key Stage 4 (post-14 education). Otherwise drama remains incidental in the English curriculum as it is not a standalone statutory subject (DfE, 2013b). This does little to encourage young people to embrace, explore and learn through the dramatic form in their early to mid-education. Sadly, this is perhaps unsurprising given the hierarchical nature of educational priorities throughout the world (Robinson, 2006).

Education's primary function is to provide opportunities for holistic development for all, and this is why the arts are as important as the sciences. When children become adults they must respond to the changing demands of society by being socially and emotionally adaptable. So they need to be taught solidarity, belongingness, problem-solving and peaceful and constructive protest and resolution. Opportunities must be provided to develop cohesive groups and community membership, encourage the generation of shared values to govern such membership, allow experimentation with roles and solutions and develop cognitive, social and emotional skills. Drama offers all these benefits and more. So although drama is not compulsory, readers are encouraged to consider FT as a legitimate way of contributing to the holistic development of children.

THE SOCIO-POLITICAL IMPACT ON EDUCATION

Socio-economic pressures and recent changes to the political agenda in the UK have had a substantial impact on young people and their families. Data from the 2011 UK census show that there are approximately 12 million children in the UK, 3.5 million of whom live in relative poverty (Whitham, 2012). Relative poverty in the UK is defined as being where 'resources are so seriously below those commanded by the average individual or family that they are, in effect, excluded from ordinary living patterns, customs and activities' (Townsend, 1979: 31). This may include poor housing conditions, overcrowding and inadequate clothing or food. Cooper and Dumpleton (2013) estimated around 500,000 people now access food banks on a regular basis in the UK, a 170 per cent increase in less than 12 months (The Trussell Trust, 2013). Furthermore, the Social Mobility and Child Poverty Commission (2014) confirmed that the UK's statutory targets to reduce child poverty will be missed and that the number of UK children in relative and absolute poverty will rise significantly by 2020. This will increase inequality, inequity and educational and social marginalization.

Despite such socio-political pressures, children are expected to arrive at school ready to learn. Yet we know that deprivation is a significant contributory factor in low educational outcomes (DCSF, 2009) and that children from low socio-economic families are more likely to have speech- and language-related difficulties (Fernald *et al.*, 2013; Perkins *et al.*, 2013). Research has shown clear links between literacy and language development (Locke *et al.*, 2002) and between language difficulties and challenging behaviour (Clegg and Hartshorne, 2004). Supporting families and relieving them of the pressures of social deprivation and isolation, and supporting homes where there is domestic violence, family separation, parental mental health difficulties or long-term unemployment, are as important as deprivation itself (Action for Children, 2010). As such, children living in deprivation or who have substantial contextual challenges are more likely to face adversity in school. They are at greater risk of not being as ready to learn when they arrive at school as their more advantaged peers. Therefore educators are tasked with preparing children for learning as well as teaching the curriculum.

Simultaneous with the onset of these socio-political developments, the central government has removed the Context Value Added (CVA) measure from Ofsted inspection criteria. The CVA measure takes a school's social context into account when deciding how well it is performing. All children need their schools to set high aspirations and provide high quality teaching but children start from different social positions, and contextual factors will influence their progress at school. The removal of CVA means that inspection procedures no longer fully take this into account. This change fails to recognize how some children may not arrive at school ready to learn, by virtue of their circumstances. Moreover, all children, regardless of their socio-economic status, are assumed to start from the same baseline, and so potentially vast inequalities and inequity between communities and individuals are created. This is more so the case for our poorest and most vulnerable children and families as the impact of welfare reforms takes hold. More than ever, the teacher's role is as much about nurturing and supporting families to meet basic needs as it is about teaching the curriculum and increasing attainment; without the former, the latter is an incredibly difficult task – an issue overlooked by the removal of CVA.

Good education engages children as active learners and is not a passive experience in which they are simply expected to retain information imparted by knowledgeable adults. Children must be empowered to use their own context and experiences so they are enabled to take ownership of their learning (Freire, 1993). With a busy curriculum and innumerable socio-political forces impacting directly on frontline services, teachers may feel that FT would just be yet another task to undertake. After all, drama is not going to eradicate negative contextual factors. However, high quality FT projects and similar drama encounters do allow children a form of expression, communication and exploration that is contextually relevant to them. Furthermore, FT offers a holistic and child-centred approach by which communities can be encouraged to identify potential solutions with stakeholders from local government and schools and effect change.

The research context
This book examines the psychological and educational qualities of FT through practical evidence-based examples and anecdotes. The FT projects featured and exercises used took place in various settings including schools, pupil referral units, community centres, community mental health settings, theatres, art centres and further education and higher education institutions. The focus is on two evidence-based examples of FT that took place in a primary school in the UK and that show how the qualities of FT can be utilized by readers in their own setting: the Transition Project and the Empathy Project. The Transition Project focused on challenges arising for children during the transition from primary to secondary school and the Empathy Project on the role of self-esteem and empathy within the FT process.

The ethos of the school where the projects took place can be best described as warm, inclusive and supportive of wider contextual issues. The setting offered wrap-around services such as after-school clubs and actively encouraged child participation. The school was set close to a military base, so mobility was high.

The Transition Project

Children and teachers from across the school were consulted on how the project should be run and the theme to adopt. Seven children from Year Six (Y6) took part in five two-hour drama-based workshops. The aim was to provide them with the necessary skills to create a play around the theme of transition and to perform the play in the style of FT. The workshops were facilitated by the author of this book, who is both a theatre practitioner and psychologist.

The decision to use untrained children as actors, rather than a professional touring company, was risk-assessed and deliberate. I believe that children can develop and run their own FT projects, and these projects made this evident. I provided high quality input to support the children to create their own play; this was an organic process that generated authentic representations of the challenges that were important to the children. In this sense the approach was context- or group-driven – the children led on the content, based on what was relevant to their concerns and experiences.

In contrast, touring theatre companies often arrive with pre-determined plays, much as Boal (1995) did. These plays may have a Personal, Social, Health and Economic education (PSHE) focus such as bullying, racism or drug awareness, and the content may resonate with the audience and be linked to curriculum objectives. However, they are unlikely to be context-specific in the same way as is achieved when working with children to develop their own play. Touring FT work is generally created for children in a range of settings, not *with* them in a specific setting. After such plays, children may have the opportunity to participate in workshops to extend their learning and make the content more relevant to contextual issues; this approach is curriculum-driven.

These two approaches are different but both are valuable, and choice between the two will invariably depend on the various needs, budgets, logistics, circumstances and philosophical positions concerned. The important point is that the facilitator should have the prerequisite skills, described earlier, to ensure high quality input.

Returning to the present work, each workshop started with warm-up exercises to prepare the children for drama-based activity. The group then focused on the theme and used theatre activities and games to develop a play. Toward the end of the block of workshops, the children were introduced to, and rehearsed, the conventions of FT. This included improvising suggestions from the audience and answering questions in character during hot-seating.

The play focused predominantly on the transition to secondary school. But because the school served a military base, transition to different countries and moving home were also common; and some children associated the work with emotive transitions, such as divorce. It would be untrue to claim that adult direction did not in any way detract from, or alter, the play or interventions but my editing was very limited and was as collaborative as possible, usually through discussion and trying out different ideas in the workshops.

The resultant play consisted of three vignettes – or short scenes – held together by a talk show narrative and shown to the entire school. The main characters were brought onto the stage by the presenter of the talk show, played by one of the children. Each vignette group was asked to show their story to the audience, as follows:

> **Story one:** A child – the protagonist – joins secondary school in Year Seven (Y7). He is intimidated by the orientation task he faces and feels lost. The child is then bullied by a Year Nine (Y9) pupil – the antagonist – who first spots the Y7 lost in the corridor.

> **Story two:** A group of girl students move from primary to secondary school together. A new child starts at the new school who has no friends from primary school. She tries to join the group of girls who transferred together, but is rejected by the group's leader. Initially, the new girl is seen as the protagonist. However, through the process of hot-seating, the group leader becomes seen as the protagonist because the spect-actors feel the group leader was challenged by her own internal anxieties lest she might lose her old friends if new people joined the group.

> **Story three:** Two friends in primary school apply to the same secondary school. One gets into her chosen school, the other child doesn't. The successful applicant responds to the news with excitement, showing little regard for her friend. This leads to a fall-out between the two. It was originally decided that the antagonist in this scenario should be the child who was successful in her application, because of her disregard for her friend's feelings. However, on deeper reflection other, more abstract challenges were identified, such as the school selection and appeals system, as well as the response of parents.

The audience was made up of peers from Reception class upwards, class teachers, the head teacher and invited adults including parents, school governors and representatives from the local authority. The children in the audience engaged with discussion, debate, hot-seating and role reversal – these were our spect-actors. The teachers and head teacher acted as Auxiliary Jokers (Hammond, 2013). The Auxiliary Joker's role is as an assistant facilitator, helping to manage the audience and supporting the contributions of children who have softer voices or those who lack the confidence to step forward. This role may be performed by a teacher, as in this case, but may also be taken by a child. The other adults in the audience were observers of the process, but did not actively participate. The play and the forum elements – referred-to collectively as the performance – were filmed with two cameras and the films were later analysed for research purposes.

After the play was run, the facilitator discussed each scene with the spect-actors. The purpose was to clarify the issues the spect-actors thought were most pressing and who they felt the protagonist was and why. Finally, the spect-actors were given the opportunity to choose which story they would like to try to resolve first. The chosen scene was re-run using the usual FT conventions, such as stopping the action, asking questions and swapping roles to overcome the challenge.

Focus groups took place within a week of the final play. Three groups were identified: children from Y6 who participated as actors; children from a selection of other year groups who made up the spect-actors; and the teachers and head teacher of the school. These focus groups were later analysed for research purposes.

The Empathy Project

The aim of this FT project was to follow-up on some of the questions raised by the Transition Project, with a particular focus on the role of empathy in the FT process. Boal (1979) discusses empathy at length in relation to the media, including theatre, television and film. For this reason empathy was identified as an important concept for further exploration. The Empathy Project was organized as a supplementary case to the Transition Project.

A different group of children from Year Five (Y5) at the same school took part in a half-day FT workshop. The workshop included the same features as the Transition Project but took less time. The children had participated in a number of FT experiences by the time the Empathy Project started and thus knew how FT worked; the workshop therefore focused on refreshing skills alongside developing a play. There is a need to invest in the initial development of FT, but when it is used periodically, subsequent

FT projects can be realized with a shorter preparation time. The play was more traditional, having four distinctive scenes and no additional narrative framework (such as that of the talk show used in the Transition Project). The play can be summarized as follows:

> Mary was known as the school bully. She had no friends and took a particular dislike to Patrick, a younger student in school. One day Mary saw Patrick reading a book intended for much younger readers. She approached Patrick and knocked the book out of his hand. She walked away laughing. Later that day Patrick told his brothers and they retaliated by picking on Mary. As the play progressed we discovered that Mary had a lot of difficulties at home, which may have been a reason for her difficulties in school.

The play was shown to Key Stage 2 (KS2) pupils, the class teacher and the head teacher. The play was run, discussed and then re-run using the same FT conventions as the Transition Project. Actors and spect-actors were asked to complete questionnaires on self-esteem and emotional literacy at the start and end of the day. Follow-up questionnaires were used one week later. A random selection of children were asked to participate in a focus group too. These data were analysed to explore further the efficacy of FT on emotional development.

Using this work to inform other contexts

Many readers may be wondering whether the work discussed here can be used in their own settings. The short answer is yes, absolutely! However, context is important and the task in the Transition and Empathy projects was to bring to life the processes inherent to FT; this was achieved partly by identifying the underlying qualities within the school that enabled the FT to be experienced positively. These qualities included the warm, inclusive and innovative setting and the school ethos. In addition, there was an experienced facilitator who had the kind of qualities discussed earlier. The more supportive qualities there are in your setting, the more likely you will be to have a successful FT project. The FT process can be further explained through theatrical and psychological theory, and these theories are now outlined.

The psychology of FT

An abundance of psychology is inherent to the process of FT. By understanding and utilizing psychological processes we can ensure the work is safe and that outcomes are optimized.

In the FT process a number of children will be selected to form the actor group and take part in workshops to develop a play around the agreed theme. Selection could be random, with names drawn from a hat, for instance, or targeted, as was the case with the Y6 pupils in the Transition Project; your chosen selection method will depend on your purpose. During drama activities the children will project their own worries, hopes, dreams, anxieties and concerns onto the developing characters and story of the play. This process, known as externalization (White and Epston, 1990), works by turning the issue into something external from ourselves. Externalization is the key psychological process used in the workshops in which children are creating their own plays. In the example of transition, children already have worries, anxieties and hopes about the transition to secondary school, and addressing these directly could feel unsafe or threatening. By allowing them to explore the theme through play, such as theatre activities, they are empowered to share their inner feelings and thoughts through carefully constructed characters and scenarios. This allows a safe space to be created in which concerns can be raised and approached indirectly.

By the end of the workshops the group would have created a play that ends with a challenge for the protagonist that is contemporary and meaningful for the spect-actors. A play with these qualities should simultaneously resonate with spect-actors and also make any challenges related to the theme tangible. At the end of the workshops and the first run-through of the play, the original challenge should still feel unresolved. Although this can feel rather uncomfortable for both the children and adults it is a very important part of the experience and one must have absolute faith in the process. It works because seeing elements of ourselves in the play creates an emotional response that makes us want to attempt change for the protagonist: spect-actors connect emotionally to the art and are provoked to act.

The feeling of discomfort before attempting transformation is a central idea to the paradoxical theory of change (Beisser, 1970). We can only make meaningful change once we appreciate where we are starting from. In other words, change can only occur once we take the time to be what we *are* as opposed to what we *want* to be (Beisser, 1970). So for the Transition Project, recognizing anxieties and challenges associated with moving school was important in order to stimulate the children to make meaningful attempts at change. Simply working on the theme 'I want to make friends in secondary school by being nice to everyone' is less fruitful because we miss out where we are. Our real emotions are in danger of being overlooked and this could make transition an even more difficult process for some children. The children's stories have already been externalized, so they recognize elements of the play and the characters' plight as being resonant to them, rather than *being* them and their own dilemmas. A well-planned and managed FT project will hold the uncomfortable negative feelings safely and guide the children to a more desirable ending.

Only at this stage are the children encouraged to move toward finding solutions for our protagonist. Through hot-seating, discussion and role-swapping they can actively try out ideas to help overcome the protagonist's challenge. Careful questioning by the facilitator encourages the children to draw on past successes and try out novel ideas in a safe rehearsal space. Psychologists refer to this process as solution-focused rehearsal (De Shazer and Dolan, 2007). The facilitator can use what we call the 'miracle question' (ibid.: 37), asking children what would happen in the scene if a miracle were to occur or if they had a magic wand. The idea is to encourage the children to collectively share experiences, creative ideas and possible solutions.

I have outlined the FT process from workshops through to the end of a performance – encompassing both the play and the forum elements. Within that process I have identified three key psychological frameworks: externalization, the paradoxical theory of change and solution-focused rehearsal (Figure 1.1).

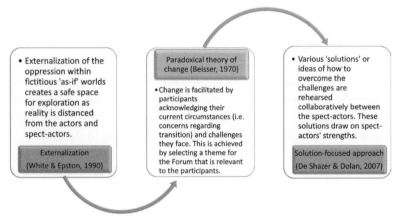

Figure 1.1: Core psychological frameworks of forum theatre

There are a number of peripheral psychological processes embedded in FT too. The process is child-centred: the start and end-point of a project where children develop their own play is the children themselves. They are encouraged to take on the roles of others and through doing so they can develop empathy. These ideas form part of what psychologists call person-centred approaches (Rogers, 1951).

But role play is not only useful for developing empathy; many psychologists also believe interacting with our environment is an important way of stimulating cognitive processes. Traditional models of cognition explain a process of input–output: children receive information from the outside world and store this information in their minds to use at a later date. Another way of seeing cognition is that our brain, body and environment are interconnected: acting on our environment has an impact on our thinking, problem-solving, reasoning and information-processing. This is a psychological–philosophical model called embodied cognition (Shapiro, 2011; Clark, 1997) that may also help trigger memories of past solutions and develop new ideas for later use through play and active problem-solving.

Ideally, children will leave FT with more ideas about how to overcome their challenge than they did before it began. All challenges are different, even if they present in a similar way. For example, if our car were to break down we might open the bonnet and change a component; on this occasion the car might be fixed. But if we broke down again, the same approach may not work; the problem looks similar, but the cause is different. This analogy can be transferred to any situation – bullying, making friends, gang membership and so on. So it is helpful to have lots of different ideas to increase the chances of finding a solution, whatever life throws at us. De Bono calls this expansion of ideas problem-solving repertoires (De Bono, 1970: 246).

FT builds these repertoires by presenting children with a well-defined problem that has restricted starting points (that is, a problem in which there are factors that limit the possibility of obvious or simplistic solutions). For instance, the central character may be experiencing bullying and may well have exhausted the obvious solutions, such as telling the teacher, before the play concludes. The spect-actors must now try to help the protagonist within the limitations of the play by generating a range of creative ideas to tackle what De Bono calls the artificial mechanical problem (De Bono, 1970: 245). This type of problem is often manufactured by a person – hence, artificial – and involves moving through staged action to resolve the problem – hence, mechanical. FT uses this approach a little more abstractly and for less trivial matters than De Bono originally intended. For instance, in FT the problem is not focused on an object such as a ladder, nor is the problem necessarily mechanical such as how to manoeuvre a long ladder from a small room (De Bono, 1970). However, the key elements of the idea are still highly relevant: a problem is created through limited starting points constructed by the play and, through initial discussions with the spect-actors, the solutions are transferrable and they can lead to developing problem-solving repertoires (ibid.: 246).

The challenge for the facilitator is to question and, to a point, play devil's advocate. In the process more solutions are demanded from the spect-actors. This increases the number of possible solutions the children have access to when faced with a similar problem in reality. In FT, the children are able to examine the same problem from different points of view, in close detail. In doing so, they gather insight leading to the likelihood of more realistic and practical solutions. Psychologists refer to this part of the process as parallel thinking:

> Parallel thinking means that at any moment everyone is looking in the same direction ... in parallel thinking, both views, no matter how contradictory are put down in parallel ... at all times the emphasis is on designing a way forward.
>
> (De Bono, 1986: 4)

The essence of FT, then, is to provide children with the opportunity to rehearse for reality (Boal, 2002). There is a school of thought in psychology that considers human beings as naive scientists. Personal construct psychology (Kelly, 1963), or PCP, claims that human beings hold views of their world unique to each person; one's experiences allow for these views to be tested and re-tested for accuracy over time and, as such, they are subject to change. For example, a child may believe that he is not very good at literacy. He may hold this view for a whole range of reasons: maybe he reads aloud to the class inaccurately or struggles to complete classroom spellings. The child tests this view in regular literacy lessons in which he continues to struggle, so forms the opinion that 'literacy is a horrible subject and I'm not very good at it'. However, if we can provide constructive experiences of literacy success over time, the child can be supported to view his world differently. This might be something like 'literacy is tricky, but I have adequate coping strategies to achieve it'.

In our FT project the children's anxieties around transition – their views of the world – were represented in the play. In this approach children are provided with a safe space in which to experience, through rehearsal, alternative views of the same anxiety-provoking situation. This rehearsal allows children to leave feeling more optimistic and with at least the start of an alternative world view. They have reached a point where they feel encouraged to attempt change in real life (Boal, 2002).

A typical FT performance is busy; children are swapping roles and sharing their ideas, but not all will participate in this way. One might assume these quieter children may not be getting anything from the experience, but this is not the case. We have known for years that observation is a form of active participation and a powerful mode of learning; psychologists call it the social learning theory (SLT). Many studies have demonstrated this phenomenon, the most infamous being that of researchers Bandura, Ross and Ross (1963). They found that children who were exposed to violent cartoons and films were much more likely than those who were not to express aggressive play behaviour during follow-up observations.

Thus the wider psychological processes inherent within FT include five additional psychological frameworks: person-centred approach, embodied cognition, PCP, problem-solving repertoires/lateral thinking and SLT (see Figure 1.2). I have touched on how, collectively, these processes might explain how FT can support emotional, social and cognitive development, and they are revisited at the relevant stage of the process throughout this book.

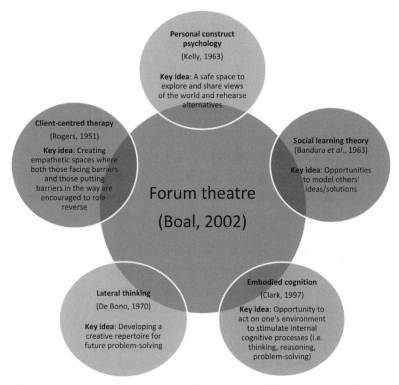

Figure 1.2: Peripheral psychological frameworks of forum theatre

A brief introduction to the theory of FT

In considering the theatrical explanation of the FT process we begin with the preparation for the play. Boal starts this exploration with the physical space within which the play will take place; he called this the aesthetic space. This could be anywhere but is likely to be a non-traditional space within community settings, such as a classroom, sports hall, corridor, youth centre, park, community centre, voluntary sector venue and so on. FT is broadly unconventional; as well as the traditional space it is not uncommon for lights, scripts, make-up, props, costumes and sets to be omitted too. If you do wish to use traditional elements it is best to recruit children from outside the actor group or those who do not wish to participate in the drama to make props, sets or costumes.

One convention worth moving away from, especially with children, is the idea of scripted text; instead we use a model of the play. Unlike a script, a model does not rely on stage direction or an abundance of words. It is a list of simple instructions such as: X happens, followed by Y, followed by Z. In the Transition and Empathy projects we used drawings to show the same outline. Figure 1.3 shows a first draft section of a model used for the Transition Project rehearsals – the word 'bridge' is used to indicate the part of the play that was part of the talk show narrative framework and not part of a vignette.

Using the model reduces the feeling of having to get the play 'right'. Removing the sense of right and wrong allows children to remain flexible and spontaneous, enabling them to be in their bodies and not stuck in their heads.

There may be a number of actors in the play, but there are always two key roles: the protagonist and the antagonist. The protagonist is the central character who faces the challenge. The choice of actor for this role may be decided in the workshops, but the children should be warned and prepared, as the spect-actors may well identify an alternative protagonist. Meanwhile, the antagonist is the character presenting the challenge to the protagonist. The antagonist could be a person such as a bully, an internal psychological force such as the protagonist's own thoughts and feelings, or even a system or other challenge represented in a symbolic or metaphorical way. Internal antagonists are likely to be the most confusing here – how do we represent thoughts and feelings? It can be achieved implicitly, through suggestion or audience interpretation of the character's actions, or explicitly by, for instance, introducing additional characters or video or audio recordings that represent the protagonist's internal processes.

Introduction of Anchor: Jeff Reed, the talk show host.

Introduction of theme: 'Transition' picture cues – caterpillar turning into a butterfly, small to big school, moving country/house, or moving year groups.

Story one: Rosie is distraught that she will be losing her best friend, Sophie. She feels jealous that she didn't get into the prestigious school that Sophie got offered a place at.

Bridge: Anchor might ask some questions to clarify the story and then introduces story two.

Story two: Olivia is in Year Seven and is feeling a little lost in this new school. She is being bossed around by a Year Nine in the corridor and is worried about being bullied.

Bridge: Anchor might ask some questions to clarify the story and then introduces story three.

Figure 1.3: Example forum theatre model on the theme of transition

Illustrations © Cindy Tatum

The aim of the FT play is to evoke an emotional reaction from the spect-actors. This will be the catalyst that propels the spect-actors into swapping roles and discussion and is referred to by Boal as the affective dimension. Without this dramatic emotional connection, the spect-actors are unlikely to be encouraged to attempt change and the FT would be likely to fall flat. Psychologists such as Fagan and Shepherd (2006) have argued that it is this emotional connection to any art form that makes an arts experience worthwhile. So the story between the protagonist and antagonist must be believable, accessible and relevant.

The play is presented in a fictitious, as-if world, within which belief is suspended – what Boal calls plasticity. The spect-actors are able to see that the space is safe, flexible and changeable. Once the play has finished, the facilitator opens discussions with the spect-actors about what has been seen; after these initial discussions the play is begun again but this time the spec-actors are invited to shout 'Stop!' at any point where they feel the protagonist is facing a challenge and requires an intervention to reach a more desirable outcome. This is the spect-actor's opportunity to imagine a world without oppression and rehearse for change. The only rule, at least initially, is that the spect-actor can swap roles only with the protagonist.

Meanwhile, the actors remain with their characters' motivations and so attempt to reduce the spect-actor's success at making changes. The process demands that the actors respond to what the spect-actor is suggesting, especially the actor playing the antagonist. The actor must remain mindful of the motivation of the character in the play and consider what would, and would not, be a realistic change. Much of this will be rehearsed during the workshop stages, but it is useful when working with children as actors to use a technique called the huddle. Once a spect-actor has shouted 'Stop!' and swaps places with the protagonist, the facilitator will go into a huddle with the relevant actor or actors and follow these steps:

1. Clarify what the suggestion from the audience member was.
2. Remind the performers that reactions should remain realistic. The aim is for the actor to not simply be agreeable to the spect-actor's suggestion for a solution.
3. Help the children reconnect with their characters' motivations – offering simple prompts.
4. Reduce any anxiety over uncertainty about what the actors need to do and reinforce the idea of the model: we only need communicate the essence of the suggestion and in that sense there is no right or wrong in how to play out a response.

The workshops, as we will see, focus on developing responses to spect-actor suggestions so the children will be well-versed in what to do. The vast majority of children are not only keen but really good at improvising with spect-actors. Remember, the actors have invested a lot of time in their play and many take great care to understand their roles. The huddle is thus a simple way of reinforcing the skills the children have already acquired and helping them prepare for improvisation.

FT should not just be a process of posing a challenge and finding a quick solution. This is unrealistic and a slick resolution will be of little use in reality. Say, for example, that Joe, our antagonist, is bullying James, that this is reported to a teacher and that the bullying stops. This solution fails to mimic the complexities of the real world and is unlikely to provide a sustainable way forward. The facilitator must play devil's advocate in order to stretch the spect-actors through discussion, debate and action, in order to explore several possible solutions. That way the spect-actors are more likely to leave with a greater chance of succeeding in overcoming the real-life challenges they might face. This part of the performance is referred to as the forum. An Auxiliary Joker usually sits among the spect-actors to offer gentle encouragement and support to enable contributions from all spect-actors (Hammond, 2013). Utilizing an Auxiliary Joker in both the Transition and Empathy projects ensured that children as young as 4 years old were able to participate fully.

To complete the picture we need to know what happened during the preliminary discussions, debate and role reversal. The facilitator is interested in helping the spect-actors identify the challenges most pertinent to them. Using the play, the facilitator highlights hidden aspects of emotion, action and words so the scenario is magnified for the children to explore the challenge in fine detail – magnification that Boal calls telemicroscopic. What was it that made Joe appear to be bullying James? How might our protagonist be feeling or thinking? How are our characters positioned in terms of body language? Furthermore, the play will represent something different for each participant; what is of importance to one spect-actor may not be so to another – a school playground may induce happiness in one participant, anger in another and anxiety in a third. What was it that Joe actually did, said or felt that characterized the act as bullying? The spect-actors may agree that the act was indeed bullying, but the detailed view of the spect-actors is not so obvious. Boal uses the term 'projection' to describe how spect-actors place their own feelings and thoughts onto the space, character or scenario. This is similar to the process of externalization described in relation to the workshops and it is where telemicroscopic elements can be really helpful.

The play – or vignettes that make up the play – is likely to run for around five to ten minutes. The forum – where the play is re-run and alternatives are rehearsed – will run for a pre-agreed amount of time. The whole performance – the play and the forum section – should last between one and two hours. Adults are invariably surprised at how well children focus and engage; even the children who generally fidget, misbehave and lose focus regularly surpass adult expectations.

At the end of the allotted time the FT play is re-run from the start with some of the most successful ideas added-in by the actors. During this re-run the spect-actor's role is to watch the constructive impact of their suggestions and they have no further opportunity to stop the action. The facilitator can discuss the final play briefly with the spect-actors afterwards to reinforce the positive outcomes they have achieved. But how do the actors, the untrained children, come up with a new play incorporating the ideas suggested by the spect-actors? The answer is the huddle. At the end of the allotted forum time, the actors all gather in a huddle and briefly discuss (1) what suggestions will be integrated into the new, more desirable, play and (2) what the structure of this new play will be.

Again, this process should not be new to the children as they will have rehearsed these skills many times over in workshops. The problem emerges where the workshops have not been adequately planned to be sure the children feel confident with the FT process. Having worked with many children using FT, I have not found any child to be overwhelmed by, or unable to participate in, this process. The trick is to ensure that the preparation for everyone involved is thorough and understood by all.

Chapter 2

The workshops

I felt that the workshops were, kind of, they made me feel like I was in control, well, not in control, but had the same kind of, everybody had the same kind of leadership as everybody else. So everybody could do what they wanted. You could put, like, everybody listened to each other and everybody listened, and I listened to everybody else.

(Y6 forum theatre participant)

Purpose: To create a safe space so that the group of children selected as actors can develop the necessary skills to develop and perform a piece of FT.

Preparing for the workshops

Working with children as actors takes careful planning and preparation, a skilled facilitator and a supportive setting. Get these right and the FT project should be safe, efficient and effective.

An FT project starts with the recruitment of key stakeholders: adults such as the head teacher, service managers and teachers and the children you propose to work with. You may wish to work on a specific PSHE issue or a specific group, such as children who present as hard-to-reach. The theme could be virtually anything from managing finances to seeking asylum, developing friendships or challenging racism. What is important is to ensure that the theme is decided *with* the children and not *for* them. The Transition Project began with a discussion with the head teacher and a randomly selected group of children from across the school. You might adopt other democratic mechanisms in your setting, such as the school council.

Ideally, these preliminary discussions will be conducted by someone who does not know the children well, so they feel they can be open about their views. Avoid picking children simply because you know they will be agreeable. These discussions should aim to introduce the concept of FT and take account of certain matters, for instance:

- Is FT something the children would be interested in taking part in?
- Would children be more interested in being in the actor or spect-actor group?
- Which year group or selection of children would be most appropriate for this kind of work?

- What kinds of issues would the children like to explore through FT?
- What other issues do the children think need considering before running the FT project?

These questions are not fixed. From discussions with the children you should be able to determine a broad, over-arching theme that is relevant to your population. Using visual prompts, drawings or video examples might help make the ideas accessible to younger children.

The theme

When working with children the theme should be broad enough to allow flexibility but narrow enough to make it manageable, so transition is a good choice. It encompasses many life events, such as moving school, house or country – and even growing up. Most children would have already experienced transitions so can understand the theme.

Projects where the theme genuinely resonates with the children are the most powerful. Some contextualization may be needed by the project leader, such as preparation in subjects such as PSHE or responding to an identified problem like bullying in the setting. In the present work, not only was school transition imminent for the Y6 pupils but many of the pupils had experienced house and school moves and had faced having to establish new friendships, adapt to new cultural values and adjust to new surroundings and circumstances.

Identifying the actor group

The next task is to determine who is to be in the actor group and who will, by default or active choice, be assigned to the spect-actor group. The actor group participates in the workshop stage of the project and engages in activities that allow participants to develop and perform their own play. The participants in the actor group could be a particular class, year group or other target group. During the preliminary discussions about the Transition Project it was democratically and unanimously decided that children from the Y6 class would form the actor group, because of their pending transition to secondary school.

What is important is that all the children face a similar challenge around the theme. The Y6 children had both transition and the context in common. The theme has to be relevant to the spect-actor group too; in this case, transition is a universally relevant topic, while other themes might not be.

Children of different ages can work together on an FT project as long as they have some common experience, background or understanding.

Children who are looked after in the care system, for instance, have a shared experience. It is easier to work with a fairly narrow range of ages to ensure a good match in their developmental abilities: do not diverge too widely.

There are a number of other factors to consider: for a start, the children should have a choice as to whether or not they wish to be in the actor group. Be aware, though, that children may say one thing and then change their minds. So let the first couple of workshops be flexible, allowing them to decide whether FT is for them. After two or three workshops, however, bringing new children into the group could disturb the dynamics unhelpfully. Also to be decided are the number of children in the actor group. Optimal numbers are around five to eight children per adult. However, where children have a learning need, behavioural difficulties or social interaction or communication needs the ratio of children to adult should be reduced.

What to do with the spect-actors

Who forms the spect-actor group will depend on your setting. In a school, your spect-actors are likely to be other pupils while parents and teachers are likely to make up the broader audience. If the project is taking place in a youth centre, drama club, as part of a voluntary project or in a community centre or arts venue, who your spect-actors and audience will be might be less clear-cut.

You might be working with a special group of children such as those who are looked after in the care system or at risk of social or educational exclusion. Or perhaps working with children around special themes such as body image or mental health. In these cases your spect-actors and audience are likely to be specially invited and not necessarily people at your setting. This is likely to be a mix of young people who have experienced similar challenges to those presented in the play, some of their parents or carers, plus adults who are stakeholders in the challenges being presented. Thus, children who have made a play in an FT project about the care system might want social workers, trainers and other local authority representatives to be invited. Children who have made a play about racism might want community development officers, police officers and youth workers to be present. Supported by the facilitator, the group decides who is invited to be the spect-actors and audience. No one should be invited whom the children do not want present, and safeguarding is the guiding principle in determining who should or should not be invited. School children may opt, for instance, to invite other pupils from their school to be spect-actors and audience, but not parents or teachers. It is useful to discuss the benefits and pitfalls of having different groups attend, and reach a group consensus. However, if the group has an impractical or unrealistic expectation (such as no teachers being present at the final performance) or it has been predetermined that people will be invited, the facilitator must, at the very outset, set down who *will* be invited to the play, making it an explicit and non-negotiable part of the contract of involvement.

In the Transition Project, the spect-actors were other pupils from Reception to Y5 and the audience made up of teachers, parents, governors and representatives from the local authority. They were only involved at the performance stage. However, if you are a teacher you may wish to include other children from the school in other roles before the play is performed, such as using art classes to design sets or props. Otherwise, the spect-actor group needs no special involvement until the performance day.

Informing parents and carers

Before the workshops can start, parents and carers will need to be informed. They need to know the answers to the following questions:

- What is FT?
- Why is FT being used?
- Why has their child been chosen to be part of the actor group?
- How long will the project last?
- Who will be leading the group?
- Who should they contact if they have a question about the FT project?

You should also decide whether guardians will need to sign a consent (opt-in) or whether their child will be included unless guardians opt out.

Careful thought does need to go into representing FT accurately to parents. It is perfectly excusable that a parent may see the word 'theatre' and think their child has been selected to perform in a traditional play. Adults may expect to see a traditional performance, and find watching the play and then the forum element a different and unexpected experience. However, adults regularly report FT as a hugely constructive experience for all the children concerned. Many parents, for example, report that FT is able to resolve conflict and support children in overcoming their lack of confidence. Reaffirming that FT is a powerful tool for change.

The workshops

The workshops in the Transition Project lasted for two hours each. Seven children took part with one facilitator over five weeks. They had previously seen a piece of FT delivered by a professional touring company but had never participated as actors. The first two workshops focused solely on a range of drama-based exercises that aimed to develop emotional awareness, memory, team work, imagination and muscular, body and sensory awareness. The exercises were designed to be fun and engaging. Some were developed from existing theatre literature such as Boal's *Games for Actors and Non-Actors*. Some were based on my own experiences as a theatre practitioner. Others were developed during the project by trying out new ideas and working with what the children brought to the space. The development of the play was not started until the third workshop. This may sound unusual but, as we will see, it serves the purpose of developing a cohesive group.

The warm-up

Each workshop starts with a warm-up session intended to prepare the children for play. The warm-up usually lasts around thirty minutes and is based on the aforementioned exercises and activities. Developing a piece of theatre demands that people are prepared mentally, physically and emotionally to engage in the challenging yet playful experience of devising. We need the children to be aware of themselves and others. We need them to focus, yet work flexibly and creatively. We need them to trust the process of creating, feel comfortable with ambiguity and be ready to play without inhibition. We want children to feel confident to share their ideas, respect others and, ultimately, perform. Children need to listen and connect both to themselves and to their character. Warm-ups are therefore essential in preparing the ground for the work that will follow.

They also help in developing a cohesive group and workable group dynamics. Members of the group will have histories among themselves that may need careful management. Before the transition workshops began I was advised that the transition process for the children I was working with had, so far, been tricky. Some had not secured places at their preferred school, which meant that, in this rural environment, they would be parting from good friends. This had caused some friction in the group. In another FT project I ran some years earlier in an inner-city school, some of the children arrived showing fierce hostility toward each other. Many had bullied or been bullied by others in the group. Now these children were having to work on a joint enterprise, face-to-face. Tension in the group was electric. The focus initially was less on making a performance than on conflict-management and resolution. So although the warm-up was our starting point for each session it had to run for a much longer period. Making sure children feel safe in the process is crucial.

Nobody who has little experience of FT should jump in at the deep end. FT is certainly effective when the preparation is good and warm-ups are made an essential component. In the aforementioned FT experience, which I call the Bullying Project, a different approach was needed from that for the Transition Project. We had a team of theatre practitioners working with the children in several small groups to develop theatre-based skills alongside FT-specific skills. They were then brought together as one large group of around 15 children and tasked with developing a cohesive performance for a whole-school assembly of some two hundred pupils.

Bringing the group together proved explosive: some children were carrying powerful emotions of anger, fear and anxiety from the playground. They neither trusted nor respected the others. Accusations and threats of bullying flew around and the possibility of achieving a harmonious performance appeared doomed. Though additional resources are rarely needed, we increased the adult-to-child ratio for the sake of safety and used the warm-ups to develop a sense of responsibility and care between the children and to show them that they had more in common than they thought.

While the first two workshops of the Transition Project were dedicated to warm-up activities and then went on to developing a play, in the Bullying Project the children were not ready for this approach. Accordingly, we focused on activities aimed at developing cohesion among the group. Some of the games we used for this have proved themselves over the years with many groups – including the groups involved with the Transition and Empathy projects.

Games to develop group cohesion
Don't Drop the Ball! is a simple but effective team-building exercise. The children stand in a circle. A tennis ball is thrown from one person to another until a pattern is established – person A throws to person B, person B to person C and so on. Once everyone has received and passed the ball, the ball returns to the child who started the pattern off. The ball is then passed around in exactly the same pattern as before. So the children must remember to whom they have passed the ball and from whom they have received it. The speed of the passing can be increased and more balls can be added to make the task trickier.

This game can be used to symbolize how we must all work together. Each tennis ball represents a child. Each person in the circle has a responsibility to keep each child – or tennis ball – included in the circle. If a ball is dropped, the nearest person picks the ball up and moves it back into the circle, re-establishing the original pattern. This provides a good analogy of how each child has a place and a responsibility to deliver a line, complete an action or fulfil some other role. But we need to be able to rely on each other to support and pick each other up should we fall out of the circle for any reason. In the tennis ball game we have a choice: we can pick up the dropped ball(s) and re-establish the circuit or we can choose to leave the ball(s) – with the result that the game will end there. In the process of creating theatre we also have a choice: we can help out the person who has forgotten their position or we can leave them and jeopardize the performance.

Anyone Who is also a widely used warm-up game. Firstly the children sit in a circle on chairs. There should be one chair fewer than there are children. The additional child stands in the centre of the circle. This person has to finish the sentence: 'anyone who ...'. This can be anything, as long as the statement is true for the child who is standing. If the statement is also true for others, they must get up and swap seats. For example the child in the centre of the circle could say: 'anyone who ... likes football'; so everyone who also likes football gets up and tries to find another seat. The person left standing in the middle once everyone has swapped is on. The children will generally select whom they sit next to at first but before long the seating plan becomes randomized as it is difficult to stay next to those they choose. At the same time the children begin to see that they have more in common than perhaps they first thought.

The trick to this game is to advance from simple sentences to more sophisticated ones. We may start with a sentence such as 'anyone who likes East Enders' or 'anyone who has short hair' or 'anyone who likes PE'. An adult can then start to introduce more reflective questions, for example: 'anyone who is happy when playing games' or 'anyone who feels silly when they get a question wrong'. It is easy to see how this might extend to reaching the heart of perceived conflict such as 'anyone who feels sad when someone is not nice to them'.

Giants, Trolls and Wizards is popular with both children and adults. It is a giant version of rock-paper-scissors. Firstly the children are placed into two teams – the left and right team, or something more imaginative. They are then given the following rules:

- Giants beat Wizards.
- Wizards beat Trolls.
- Trolls beat Giants.

They are also told to follow certain actions – demonstrated by the facilitator:

- Giants stand tall.
- Trolls are small.
- Wizards point their wands.

In their respective teams, the children must decide on the best strategy to beat the other team. The children may decide to all be giants, trolls or wizards. Or they may decide to randomize their characters or attempt to match their counterpart on the other team. Whatever they decide, the children have to work together to win for the team. They are given around ten seconds to confer – depending on the size of each team. Once time is up, the teams must stand in a line. A child from each team must face a child from the other team. Figure 2.1 is a simple representation of how this should look – L1, 2, 3 and so on represent the left team. R1, 2, 3 and so on, represent the right team:

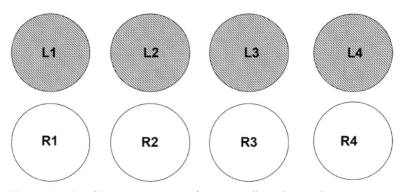

Figure 2.1: Graphic representation of giants, trolls and wizards

On the count of three everyone turns around and strikes a pose as a giant, troll or wizard. Each pair – L1–R1, L2–R2 and so on – has the opportunity to win a point for its respective team. The facilitator acts as referee. Following the rules, the facilitator must decide which child from each pair wins the point for their team. The team with the most points wins the game; the best of three rounds is usually adequate but the children often want more.

All these activities share common implicit ground rules that, when used creatively, are effective at getting people to start to work together. The games can help children play with simple characters, become aware of their space, physicality and listening, and also to focus, work in a team and care for others.

Another common difficulty when working with children is the reluctance of certain groups to work together (such as boys and girls initially being reticent about collaborating with one another). Activities such as those described can be used to break down such issues by creating an attitude of collectiveness and responsibility to complete the task in hand.

To understand the importance of warm-ups it is useful to look at some of the psychology relating to diversity and conflict management. Intergroup contact theory (Allport, 1979), for example, explains how prejudice and conflict are fostered by the way people categorize others into the in-group – usually the majority – and the out-group – usually the minority. In the FT project, rather than being openly defined, the minority out-group was simply observable because they were excluded by the majority – the in-group. In the Bullying Project the in-group comprised the children who justified their negative behaviour toward the out-group by attributing undesirable characteristics to them, such as wearing the wrong trainers. The out-group were from a different social group, lived in the 'wrong' area and generally perceived that they were the ones being bullied. If we establish groups effectively, there is likely to be a neutral group too – the group that respects the differences of the out-group, yet gets along with members of the in-group. Members of the neutral group are less likely to engage in negative behaviour toward the out-group and are important when you are trying to tackle a subject like bullying. To help ensure this balance the facilitator may, for example, want to suggest to teachers that among the children they select for the FT project there should be some who are seen as good role models in terms of managing themselves – and relationships with others – effectively. Allport (1979) suggests that the in-group and out-group should:

- have contact with each other
- have equal status within their contact
- have common goals
- have shared rules that are fair and clear
- have commonalities and the ability to celebrate diversity as constructive attributes.

These are all elements that can be used in an FT project; they provide good starting points for any group and the games are worth extending with hard-to-reach groups. The initial workshops should aim to develop the sense of cohesion, trust, responsibility and discipline needed to create and perform a piece of FT. The initial workshops can be further strengthened by:

- providing strong workshop leadership
- providing a consistent approach that is fair and transparent
- providing regular feedback to others in your setting

Nick Hammond

- using consistent positive behaviour management strategies
- stating clear expectations for children and adults – co-created ground rules are good.

Managing behaviour

Behaviour management is a priority for all settings where children and young people work and play. FT is an enjoyable and playful approach but theatre remains a discipline, requiring focus, attention, cooperation and negotiation. The children must be able to follow instructions and listen to each other to create a play. Therefore, while allowing freedom for fun and playfulness, it is essential to ensure behaviour is managed effectively, although not all groups will require contentious issues or relationships to be managed. A more common demand is that of striking the balance between drama as play and theatre as a discipline. This is particularly the case as the performance day approaches.

In addition to the strategies discussed, such as establishing ground rules and positive behaviour management – rewards, feedback for on-task behaviour and explaining what desirable behaviour would look like – everything is directed toward the final goal of creating and performing a play and engaging in activities that will enable children to develop skills such as listening and focus. The Transition Project used a wide range of activities to support children in developing these skills, including the game Chinese Movement.

Chinese Movement is similar to the classic Chinese Whispers. The children stand in a line, one behind the other. The child at the back of the line is asked to think of a movement. She then taps the shoulder of the child in front of her and shows him the movement. He then taps the shoulder of the child in front of him and attempts to replicate the same movement. This continues until the front of the line is reached where the last child turns to the group and attempts to replicate the original movement. The movements used can be very simple, such as waving, or more complex. Initially, simple movements can be useful to warm up the group but the facilitator should encourage more complex movements to stretch the group after the initial go. The task is to accurately replicate the original movement – and added sound if the group wish – at the end of the line. The facilitator encourages the children to identify the skills that will help them toward their goal such as listening, watching, concentrating and cooperating.

Re-focusing on the theme

Old and new activities continue to be used during the workshops, but now the focus shifts to exploring the theme. Children can benefit from having

34

preliminary discussions around the theme to create a word bank (a list of key ideas or words written down by the facilitator to refer back to at a later time) or mind map of key ideas related to it. We call these sub-themes. Transition might link to physical transitions such as moving school, year group, home or country. It might also represent social and emotional aspects such as leaving friends, meeting expectations over the increased complexity of academic tasks associated with the move up to secondary school or parents separating. The children in the Transition Project discussed all of these aspects and were also able to say what was meaningful to them related to the theme.

A range of practical drama activities enables the children to develop and refine their ideas further. As the workshops progress the facilitator must remain mindful that some issues may be traumatic for some children in either the actor or spect-actor group, so careful judgements must be made between exploring all sub-themes and knowing when a sub-theme might be too overwhelming. An example of a potentially traumatic sub-theme related to transition includes recent bereavement or divorce, as such life-events have the potential to evoke emotional responses that are inappropriate to explore unless the facilitator is immensely skilled and knows the child, the circumstances and the spect-actors very well. Generally, such sub-themes require attention in forums outside the FT, although facilitators do have to take measured risks and decide whether a particular sub-theme, although risky, may be appropriate and safe enough for the scope of the project.

Therapy or therapeutic?

Therapeutic approaches in the UK education system have increased over the last ten years (Ecclestone and Hayes, 2009). Recent examples include Targeted Mental Health in Schools (TaMHS) projects (DCSF, 2008) and the Children and Young People's Improving Access to Psychological Therapies (CYP IAPT) programme (Department of Health, 2011). These initiatives have seen an increase in school-based support staff such as Emotional Literacy Support Assistants, who are school-based Teaching Assistants with additional training.

In *Rainbow of Desire* (1995), Boal claimed that his methods in the Theatre of the Oppressed could be used as therapy. This is certainly not advocated here: children do not attend school, visit a youth centre, access a drama club or perform FT for therapy. Unless you are a trained therapist, in FT your intention will be entirely generic.

But I do argue that FT can be therapeutic, in the sense that participation can bring coincidental benefits. FT is not intended to be used as a treatment or intervention for emotional distress. However, children do report feeling more confident and empowered to attempt change in their own lives because of FT, and this effect has the *potential* to create desirable outcomes such as reducing the stress of transition. The major difference here is that therapy is practised by trained therapists and there is an *explicit intention* between therapist and client to reach a therapeutic end by creating insight or change (Milton *et al.* 2004; Langley, 2006). FT, meanwhile, has the *potential* to *incidentally* create change or insight through the use of drama and exploring issues of relevance to the community concerned. This may feel a little ambiguous; indeed it is a grey area reflected in the literature, where there is consensus on the ambiguity between therapy and therapeutic practice. But to be quite clear, children do not perform FT for therapy and this was not the intention behind how FT was used in this work.

Your themes will be broad and perhaps linked to PSHE. The intention of the FT is to provide a safe space in which children can explore the theme. They are enabled to explore social, emotional and behavioural components of the theme while their social and emotional development are supported. The process offers children a unique, playful experience that in these examples helped develop creative problem-solving repertoires. Certain principles are essential to ensure an FT project is successful and safe:

- Ensure you work within your own skills and capacity.
- Ensure, as much as possible, that your work will not do any harm. Only take measured risks. This can be achieved by talking to others in your setting, working within your own professional code of ethics and trusting your experience and observation.
- Ensure you have feedback processes in place. Peer and management supervision can be helpful. If you are a visitor to a setting, identify a link person there.
- Ensure you have an aftercare plan. This is explored fully in Chapter 4.
- Ensure you have clearly defined boundaries. Many people working with children are used to creating and maintaining boundaries. If you have a dual role – such as a teacher and workshop facilitator – consider what the differences and similarities are between those roles. How will you communicate the differences in these roles to the children?
- Ensure the facilitator is clearly identifiable and takes leadership on managing the process: the facilitator is the person in charge, the person who provides containment, leads the group and makes decisions on the group's direction.

- Ensure group members are assessed for readiness. Ground rules should be based on shared values and should include a 'bottom line' response such as, at what point will the work stop if there is persistent off-task behaviour?
- Ensure as far as possible that the facilitator has the confidence, experience, skill and external resources to explore a given theme. Are there follow-up plans in place, should a theme or sub-theme unintentionally prove traumatic?

The guiding rule is: if the theme is not going to cause harm, go ahead. If you are in any doubt, check it out. However, certain themes and sub-themes are always off-limits, such as when they represent a recent or live issue for the child – for example a divorce or bereavement – or when an identified need is currently being addressed by another agency, in which case you must check the work out first.

Finally, the facilitator needs to ensure the physical space is large enough and suitable for the proposed work. You will need to move around so having fixed tables and chairs in your space, for example, would be inappropriate. That said, you have to start with the resources you have, and from small beginnings great adventures can flourish. A notable example is the child-led arts project called Room 13 that started in a Scottish primary school. It began in a disused cupboard but as it became more successful the school managed to find a suitable, long-term space and Room 13 became an international success (Room 13 International, 2012).

Developing character

Developing strong multi-dimensional characters is essential to a good story. Character development can be supported in a number of ways. All the FT projects mentioned used a combination of theatre games, props, costume, pictures, sounds, poems and stories as projective tools. These tools are brought to life through imagination and play, such as creating new worlds within which the character lives and experimenting with props or costume to feel how the character's physicality, voice or motivations change. Throughout the process children are encouraged to become the characters they are developing and answer questions in role from others in the group. This helps to explore the motivations, thoughts and feelings of the character. During character development write the name of the child's character on a sticky label for them to wear when in character. The use of the sticker becomes even more important during the de-role phase (discussed in Chapter 4).

I use the Yeti Language exercise early on in character development with groups. The game requires two volunteers: someone to play the Yeti and someone to play the Interpreter. The other children in the workshop sit in the audience as interviewers. The roles are simple:

> **The Yeti** is invited to sit on a chair in front of the group. She must respond to questions in gibberish – her own made-up nonsense language.

> **The Interpreter** is invited to sit on another chair in front of the group. His job is to translate what the Yeti is saying into the language of the group.

> **The Interviewers** are the other children in the workshop. Their job is to find out as much about the Yeti as possible by asking questions.

Once the roles are established the workshop facilitator introduces the Yeti's back story. This story can be tailored to your theme – in the case of transition, for example, you might say that the Yeti has migrated from the mountains where she used to live and is newly arrived in the children's town. The floor is opened up to questions from the interviewers. In the Transition Project interviewers asked all sorts of questions: 'what is your name?', 'why did you decide to leave your home?', 'do you have any family and friends?' and so on. The interviewers ask questions they feel are relevant. The Yeti would answer in gibberish and the Interpreter would translate for the group.

Although the Yeti responds, it is the Interpreter who provides the understandable answer, so we are actually accessing the views of the child who is playing the Interpreter. For example:

> **Interviewers:** How do you feel about moving to a new school?

> **Yeti:** *Responds in nonsense language*

> **Interpreter:** Yeti feels excited about moving, but will really miss her friends.

The child playing the Interpreter has no idea what the Yeti is saying any more than the interviewers do but is forced to respond in character by the parameters of the game. So he gives an answer based on his own thoughts, feelings, experiences and expectations. The children are beginning to *externalize* their anticipation of transition into the safety of drama.

However, Yeti Language is also a profound way of exploring social justice – equality, empowerment, voice, belonging, community cohesion, sustainability, power distribution and power imbalance. These concepts are important to FT but also in everyday life. If a child is bullied she may feel disempowered, voiceless and reasonably feel a sense of unfairness. Yeti Language is a great exercise to introduce these complex and philosophical concepts to children. Questions arise, such as:

- Who is the interpreter?
- Who has given this person the power to respond on behalf of the Yeti?
- Was this person volunteered or democratically elected?
- Can we trust the interpreter? Why or why not?
- Has the interpreter changed what the Yeti was saying? How much?
- What is the interpreter's agenda?

Explain to the children that the questions are not directed at the child playing the Interpreter but that the character is representative of power figures. Figures in the Transition Project included parents, teachers and representatives of the appeals system. Other figures that can be used include: the bully, school systems, social care systems and political structures and representatives of those systems such as politicians or service managers for example. Here the children, if they are developmentally mature enough, are introduced to characters representing abstract ideas; in the case of the group of Y6 children who worked on the Transition Project, they were articulate and perceptive and could work with such subtleties. In my experience, most children from the age of nine should be able to access such ideas with relative ease. Most will be able to offer insight into what it is like to play the Yeti and the Interpreter. After the game is finished, we can ask questions that will allow the children to reflect in less abstract terms:

- How did you feel being the Yeti? The Interpreter? The interviewers?
- Did you [the child playing the Yeti] feel your views were represented accurately?
- How might the voice of the Yeti be misinterpreted, misrepresented, understated, overstated or without emotion?

Yeti Language is a flexible game that can be used to introduce a number of important FT skills such as hot-seating, improvisation and exploration of power, voice and challenge.

Another excellent character development tool used in the FT projects is tableau work. Tableaux can be used to create narratives and, combined with hot-seating techniques, are very effective. Each child in the group is given a number and told they will be called to the stage area by that number and, once on stage, will take up a freeze-frame position – known as a tableau

– that relates to the group's theme. Another child is called by number to join the tableau and they assume a related posture or position, thus forming a new image that links to the first one. To start with it is best to have only two or three children per tableau. Once your selected number of children are in their tableau the rest of the group are asked what they think is happening in the scene. The facilitator then presses 'play' on the scene to make the tableau come to life and the tableau children begin to improvise a scene based partly on what they have heard from the other children and partly on their own intentions when making up the original scene. From this, the facilitator then uses a host of tools to help them in the next stage, such as:

- hot-seating to develop and understand character
- allowing the non-tableau children to swap roles
- introducing new characters suggested by the non-tableau children
- allowing the tableau children to improvise a scene from their picture
- allowing non-tableau children to 'sculpt' a new picture, by directing the tableau children to move into different poses or stage locations, for example. This can be helpful when looking at body language and positioning.

The tableau work can be prompted by the facilitator through questions such as:

- What do you think is happening in this tableau?
- Who do you think the characters are? How are they related to each other?
- Is there anything you would change about the tableau?
- If we were to introduce speech bubbles, what would each character say?

Like Yeti Language, tableau work can be extremely useful to develop a range of skills the children will need later on, such as:

- improvisation and imagination
- stage positioning
- role exchange/role play
- critical thinking of character – motivation, emotion, physicality, thought
- hot-seating
- developing narrative and scenes.

The story of Sid Allen (tableau): in the Transition Project, tableau work was introduced to the group as a closing activity of one of the early workshops. All the children were asked to step one-by-one into a freeze frame. Once this tableau was completed each child stepped out in turn and was asked by the facilitator what might be happening in the scene, and through this process their story was gradually constructed. They introduced their protagonist, Sid Allen. Sid was a man who sold lottery tickets for a living and shopped at the Co-op. Sid ate a lot of beans, wore Speedos and ate pants. But Sid had a secret: he was actually an alien who was visiting earth and was confused by what he had seen and how he saw humans behave.

Within a few minutes the children, as we can see, had established an opening scene that included an interesting character and a potential back story that could be explored further. It is important to encourage the children to feel that there is no right or wrong answer. Over time they begin to trust their spontaneity, imagination and creativity. This leads to the potential of developing exciting plays with depth and breadth to the characters and stories and, most importantly, plays that are owned by the children.

There are less active ways of developing character too, such as free-writing exercises and collective drawing tasks. Exercises of this kind are useful initially to help children develop material that can later be explored through hot-seating or tableau work. Neither was used in the Transition or Empathy project, but both have been useful in other FT ventures, especially with younger children.

Broadly speaking the free-writing task is appropriate for children from the age of seven – Y3, depending on the child's confidence in literacy. In a free-writing exercise, the children are given a piece of paper and pencil. They have 60 seconds (or perhaps a little longer) to write whatever comes into their mind. The idea is for them to write down whatever comes to mind without any time to process their thoughts. This way the material is less filtered and more creative and spontaneous. Unlike the Freudian technique of free association, free writing is not intended to be analysed for personal insight – remember, FT is not therapy. Rather, this exercise provides lots of information, some of it nonsensical and some of it open to the imagination. A typical free-writing exercise is likely to generate something like this:

> Once in the moon there was a fish and in the sky lived an alien who didn't like fish. The fish had four fingers but no feet. In the garden there was a magical door and through the door lived the wizard. The girl went through the door and her wish was to visit the moon and meet the fish. She thought the fish could help with a problem she had at school.

This free-writing example is quite sophisticated. Variants of free writing can be anything from a list of words and short sentences to a more coherent piece of imaginative writing like this. In the free-writing example provided, we might consider the following questions:

- Who is the girl?
- What problem does the girl have at school?
- How could the four-fingered fish help her?
- Is this writing referencing a dream of the girl? Or her imagination? Or reality?
- Who does the garden belong to? Where is the magical door?
- Can only the girl see the magical door?
- Can the girl only get one wish from the wizard?
- Who is the alien? Does the alien not like any fish or just dislike the fish with four fingers?

This list is not exhaustive but several characters and possible stories have been generated. These stories and characters are then extended through the activities described earlier. Most children will enjoy taking part in activity of this kind even if they do not particularly enjoy writing. The task has clear boundaries and the children can choose not to share their writing.

If the children are too young, or unable or unwilling to undertake a writing task, they may be amenable to a collective drawing task. Psychologist Donald Winnicott (1971) developed an activity he called the squiggle game. The game began with a mark drawn on a piece of paper – a squiggle – and the psychologist and client took turns to extend the pattern. The squiggle game aimed to encourage play and help clients explore their own creativity and self. The collective drawing task is an extension of the squiggle game I stumbled on during one workshop. It works like this:

- A large piece of paper is placed on the wall or floor.
- A child or the facilitator draws a shape, object or character – it could be abstract or be representative of reality, but it should be distanced from the child's real story.
- The other children take it in turns to add to the picture.
- This process repeats until one of the following happens:
  o A predetermined time has been reached – a minimum of five minutes.
  o A predetermined number of rotations has been reached – a minimum of three goes each.
  o The page has been filled.

At the end of the process you should have a scene on paper. This scene may be as abstract or coherent as the free-writing task; collective drawing is a non-verbal way of similarly recording information. When the picture is complete, the children are asked a number of questions such as: Who is in the picture? What is the scene? What are the characters trying to do? Tools such as tableau and hot-seating can be employed to develop the work into a play. Although collective drawing works with young children and those with learning needs, I find it less effective with older children than collective writing.

No matter how good the characters or narrative the children develop, they need the required performance skills to put together and present their work. Children must learn the basic components of theatre – tableau, movement and speech – and become competent in all of them so they can deliver their play effectively. A simple but effective game to support this is 1-2-3. The game can also be used to develop characters for later exploration.

1-2-3 works with these basic building blocks of theatre and, again, should be linked to the theme. Firstly, the children are paired and assigned to group A or B. The pair will take turns to say the numbers one to three in turn:

A: One
B: Two
A: Three
B: One
A: Two
B: Three

This continues until the pairs have mastered the task, usually 30 seconds to a minute. The facilitator then asks the number one to be replaced with a tableau image. The children continue:

A: Gets into the position of a tableau (a freeze-frame) related to theme
B: Two
A: Three
B: Gets into the position of a tableau (a freeze-frame – the **same** image as A showed)
A: Two
B: Three
A: Gets into the position of a tableau (a freeze-frame – the **same** image as A showed)
B: Two

This continues until the pairs have mastered the task. The facilitator then asks the number two to be replaced with a simple movement or gesture, again related to the theme. The children continue:

> **A:** Gets into the position of a tableau (a freeze-frame – the **same** as before)
> **B:** Shows simple movement
> **A:** Three
> **B:** Gets into the position of a tableau (the **same** freeze-frame as before)
> **A:** Shows simple movement (the same as before)
> **B:** Three

The tableau and movements should remain the same throughout this exercise. The next step is for the number 'three' to be replaced with a word or short sentence (as before, related to the theme). The children continue:

> **A:** Gets into the position of a tableau (the **same** freeze-frame as before)
> **B:** Shows simple movement (the same as before)
> **A:** Says a word or short sentence
> **B:** Gets into the position of a tableau (the **same** freeze-frame as before)
> **A:** Shows simple movement (the same as before)
> **B:** Says a word or short sentence (the same as before)

Many children find this task tricky and it can cause some frustration as it demands a lot of focus, practice and patience to master – all important skills for performing a piece of FT live. The children are then asked to run the three components through from start to finish – this should take around ten seconds. Here is an example related to transition:

> **A:** Tableau of a child sitting down looking upset
> **B:** Puts hand on A's shoulder
> **A:** Says 'I'm OK'

We have created a very short scene with two characters: character A looks upset – why? Character B looks concerned – how does she relate to character A? Character A says he is ok, but he looks unhappy. In the Transition and Empathy projects each pair was watched in turn and the others were asked what they thought might be happening. Hot-seating the characters or asking the children to play out what might happen next is a good extension to this game.

1-2-3 provides the children with a tangible experience of using the basic building blocks of theatre and teaches them that:

- each scene must begin clean with a tableau
- pauses are not only important but in some cases very powerful
- relationships between characters need not be made explicit or literal
- clarity is gained by establishing a steady pace and using just enough movement and speech to convey the message, and no more – rather than relying on too much movement or overuse of spoken content.

Simple movements and tableaux can be more powerful than words – the facilitator should use the phrase 'don't tell me, show me'. All this leads to the process of externalization in the workshop space so that challenges are projected onto fictitious characters and stories (White and Epston, 1990) and issues can be explored from a safe distance. We begin to see elements of paradoxical change too, as the children become aware that they have certain similarities to their fictional characters. Their characters are facing transition with a range of thoughts and emotions that resonate with their real lives. The links are implicit, but the children recognize the similarities, whether or not they link their character to their own experiences.

In the Transition Project we may recall the two children who had been close friends but had fallen out because both had applied for the same secondary school and only one had been accepted. Here, a Y6 child shares the real story in a follow-up discussion after the project had ended (names and locations have been changed):

> **Y6A(2):** All the Year Six girls are going to Argyle High and Alice is going to, um, Bluebell Academy with Duncan, so she's the only girl from this school that's going and I feel sorry for her. 'Cos all the other girls, she was going to be going with Danielle but then Danielle didn't get into Bluebell Academy.

During the character development stages of the Transition Project, Alice and Danielle created a vignette that closely resembled their falling-out after only Alice succeeded in gaining a place at her preferred school. The children explained that the appeals process was not easy and that they were disappointed that taking it had changed nothing. During a follow-up discussion, the head teacher reflected on the impact the appeals process had had on the children:

> **HT:** [I think parents have] been a bit unrealistic and, um, have sort of promised more than the system's able to deliver. As I say ...

they're quite resilient children, I think they've handled it well, but with less resilient children we may well have had an awful lot more mopping-up to do than we've actually had.

The children clearly had a firm footing in their present lives and were keen to develop a play around their experience. So I suggested they might use the feelings evoked by their experiences to develop their characters' motivations and actions, and tried to discourage the replication of their real life story. Here, in the children's final vignette, Sophie (Alice) and Rosie (Danielle) are the names the children gave to their characters:

Scene one: Sophie walks onto the stage looking very pleased with herself

Sophie: Yey, yey, I got in! I got in!

Rosie: I didn't.

Sophie: Ah [Sophie turns away and whispers] I got in(!) I got in(!)

Scene two: Rosie storms onto the stage

Rosie: It's not fair! Not fair, not fair! I should have got in instead of her!

Sophie walks on stage left, stops and looks at Rosie. Rosie looks angry. Sophie continues to walk off stage right. Sophie stops and turns to the audience and addresses them.

Sophie: Hey, did you get in? I did. Hooray!

Scene changes to art class. Sophie and Rosie are sitting next to each other.

Voice off stage (teacher): Sophie, come over here please.

Sophie leaves to see the teacher (off stage right) and leaves her art work on the chair. Rosie gets up and rips up Sophie's work. After a short time, Sophie returns.

Sophie: You're supposed to be my friend. [Sophie turns to walk off stage right.]

Rosie: You're supposed to be mine.

Facilitators are tasked with supporting children in externalizing elements of reality into fictional stories and characters. The key is to be mindful of the child's real experiences, not fearful of them. After all, they have already projected elements of themselves into drama activities in the workshops. As McFarlane (2005) suggests, drama creates distance, and this allows for objectivity where the child can get closer to the experience both within the play and in real life. Done well, this is a highly beneficial part of the FT experience – as two members of staff from the Transition Project reflected during the follow-up focus groups:

> KS1CT: I think it's a good way to work through the issue rather than targeting, you know, children with the issue. So you, 'cos they're being actors and actresses ... it's not their behaviour it's the behaviour of the character, that can be dealt with.

> HT: But you know, to actually getting (in) there and take the role of a, take a role over from an actor, it made them think but also it, it moved away from, from the trauma of what had actually happened in the original scenario. And that, I can't think of anything else we do, or that's been recommended to us to do, that does that really.

These children were given an opportunity to take ownership and solve a contemporary and contextually relevant issue. Even though the original vignette ended negatively – with the children falling out over the appeal – the process of externalization ensured everyone remained at a safe distance. However, having the opportunity to share and resolve each vignette is important, as this gives spect-actors the opportunity to help the children overcome their own feelings.

Note that the challenges being presented already exist for the children, if only in their minds. So we are unlikely to be uncovering worries that were not already in the child's unconscious (Boal, 1995). Boal maintains that we only present a small part of our personality to the world and that FT can allow for exploration of one's full self. In this case, the children bring to mind – and work through – some of the potential challenges inherent in transition. FT has an element of measured risk but also offers credible opportunity:

> ... a sick personality can, in theory, try to awaken personnages, this time not with the goal of dispatching them back into oblivion but in the hope of mixing them into his personality. I am afraid, but inside me there also lives the courageous man; if I can wake him up, perhaps I could keep him awake.

> (Boal, 1995: 38)

Here Boal describes the potential of FT to stir constructive inner resources of which we may otherwise be unaware. The children become mindful of their concerns and later, in the performance section, they will rehearse possible solutions. Furthermore, as adults become more aware of the child's most pressing needs and worries they can take a proactive approach to offering appropriate support.

Developing narrative

The development of character is almost synonymous with developing narrative, since these aspects of the play run in parallel. There are alternative ways of generating stories to the character-driven ideas illustrated earlier, such as a storytelling circle. This activity begins with the children standing in a circle. One child is elected to go first, and says a single word. Going clockwise, each child adds one word. This is a great way to get stories started and goes something like this:

Child 1: Once
Child 2: Upon
Child 3: A
Child 4: Time
Child 5: There
Child 6: Lived
Child 7: A
Child 1: Beautiful
Child 2: Princess
Child 3: Who
Child 4: Had
Child 5: Everything
Child 6: Except
Child 7: For ...

The story could be based in fairy tale or relate to a reality, possibly to do with school. The content could take any direction. How many times the participants go round the story circle will vary. The idea is to have enough information to work with but not so much that creativity is stifled. It might be more useful to move on to tableau or hot-seating to explore the key characters in the story.

Hot-seating is a key tool. It can be quite tricky, as it demands that the child in the hot-seat respond on the spot and on their own. During the early workshops of the Transition Project one of the children struggled to respond to hot-seating questions and this revealed his lack of clarity around his character's motivations. I suggested that we swap him with another child to see if this made any difference. The other child took up the hot-seat position and immediately responded in a believable, emotionally engaging and dramatic way. It is helpful to allow the children to try out different roles to find the most comfortable fit. They are not trained actors, so the facilitator must guide the process.

There is no set rule for constructing the play but some basic components are essential: a beginning, a middle and an undesirable end – usually related to the challenge being shown. In the case of transition these challenges included bullying, getting lost and struggling with tricky coursework.

The play – or vignettes if you are developing several mini-plays – is likely to last between three and 15 minutes, depending on the complexity of the story, how long the workshops take, how much quality material is generated, and how much time is allocated to the FT performance section. The Transition play ran for around ten minutes. The entire FT performance – including the play and the forum – was scheduled for two hours. Three vignettes were developed, each lasting a couple of minutes. These followed a basic structure:

> **Scene one**: Establish the characters. Who are they? Where is the play set?
> **Scene two**: What background is needed for the characters? How do characters relate to each other? What happens next?
> **Scene three**: What is the challenge? Who is posing the challenge? Is the challenge from another person or internal or systemic? Who is being challenged? Why?
> **Scene four**: What next? What is the aftermath of the conflict? This has to be pessimistic and offer no resolution since it is for the spect-actors to work on a resolution.

This basic framework works well with children. Not being trained actors, they respond better to a simple presentation than to a contrived or overcomplicated plot with subtle nuances. However, you can develop a more complex play if you wish and have the available time and resources.

When using FT with children – especially where there are more than three or four in the group – my experience suggests that it is most likely that several vignettes will be developed, rather than a stand-alone play. All the children will have views and will want their ideas to be expressed in the play. Small vignettes not only facilitate this but also allow different aspects of the theme to be presented. But to hold these vignettes together it helps to use a recognizable narrative structure. The Transition play used the structure of a talk show.

A Y6 child who wasn't keen on having a bigger role played the talk show host. His role was to introduce each vignette group to the stage. He began by asking what the problem was, but before receiving a full answer, he would pause the explanation and say: 'let's have a look'. The actors would then perform their vignette to the spect-actors. This sequence was repeated until all three vignettes had been shown. Afterwards the play ran again from the start and the spect-actors had the opportunity to stop the action and attempt to help the protagonist overcome their challenge. When the vignettes were re-run, the talk show element was abandoned. The talk show is one of hundreds of potential narrative structures. You might use an alien invasion situation to discover more about bullying, a game show format to explore racism or a pirate ship adventure to understand asylum. The narrative should be accessible and easily applied, limited only by the FT group's imagination. The narrative structure should be easily recognizable, act as a vehicle to enhance the story and, importantly, simplify ideas and process, not complicate them.

Preparing for the performance

The last couple of workshops focus on getting ready to perform the work and prepare for the forum element. Be sure that the narrative structure is in place and the play is realistic, relevant and dramatic. The projects featured here were naturally child-led, as the children knew their spect-actors well, living and learning in much the same contexts. The actors also knew what was relevant to their spect-actors. Although we may have to guide children away from re-enacting scenes from movies or television soap operas – not always easy – their FT stories are usually relevant to their real lives.

The last workshop is a final rehearsal of the play where children get the opportunity to experience the game of FT as an actor and spect-actor. While each vignette group performs, the other members of the group act as spect-actors. The children take this in turn and so experience both roles. Importantly they get time during rehearsals to get the feel of what the actual performance day will be like and feel prepared by knowing their characters' motivations and emotional and behavioural responses.

The process of playing both actor and spect-actor also helps the children to learn the game of FT in which it is the spect-actor who attempts change while the actors remain in character, only changing where suggestions align to their characters' motivations. This game takes practice, but every child I have worked with has been able to achieve it, as long as it is carefully planned and the children are supported. It is certainly worth investing ample time in the preparation to secure the smooth running of the forum element on the day of the performance.

The actors should understand who the two key characters are: the antagonist, who poses the challenge to the other main character – the protagonist. As we have seen, the antagonist can be a person, such as a bully, teacher, parent; or it can be a system (or product thereof) such as the appeals system or the increase in coursework. Or the challenge might be within the protagonist, perhaps their own thoughts or feelings holding them back from being all they want to be – for instance because they think: 'I'm rubbish at making friends', and so feel socially inadequate. The challenge for the protagonist is then about what is going on with their own emotions and thoughts rather than an external antagonist such as the system or people around them.

The protagonist is the central character and the one who faces the main challenge. The spect-actors will be swapping places with this character throughout the forum in order to help them overcome their challenge. Crucially, whatever is decided in the workshops may be perceived differently by the spect-actors and is subject to change during the forum. The children should therefore be prepared and the facilitator mindful to support the actors when this occurs.

Why FT is worth the effort

Children will often be enthusiastic and dedicated and have conviction for their characters, whom they come to care for deeply. Managing reality and play is essential throughout the workshops and engaging children as actors in the workshops certainly proves to be of benefit. In the Transition Project, for example, this Y5 child who took part as a spect-actor describes how seeing her peers acting made the play realistic and accessible:

> Y5SA: ... the children could get into the same problem as what the theatre thingy, you know, and um, it would be children acting it and it doesn't really work if adults are pretending to be at school and pretending to be the children.

Using children as actors is a different experience from exposing them to theatre company productions and demands that far more time and effort be invested. Nevertheless, the teachers involved with the Transition Project valued the contribution FT makes in comparison to other approaches – as the head teacher observed:

HT: You tend to be hammering away at something but really [it] isn't there. You know, if you've given them something to work with and put right or change [inaudible], um ... then you've got a context haven't you and I think that's what worries me about Circle Time, the context is always a bit vague, you know, however many props you've got ...

The actor group found the workshops remarkably liberating. Even though FT may appear to be ambitious for 10-year-olds, the children involved as actors had this to say at the follow-up focus group discussion:

Y6A(1): I liked it how you could just put out your own, your own thoughts without anyone saying 'no, no that's wrong, that's not in the script'. I liked it how you could just make it up as you go along, not make it up ... you had to stick to [a] map, but you ...

Y6A(3): A model ...

Y6A(1): Like we're, at the moment, we're doing puppets [in a different activity, related to another subject] and there's a script and we actually have to follow the script and I'm not fussed on it.

Y6A(2): Yeah, he kept on, he kept on going wrong. It said, erm ...

Y6A(1): ... 'cos I'm bad ... I'm a bad reader...

NH: OK, so, so not sticking to a script was ...

Y6A(1): ... it was just easy 'cos ...

Y6A(2): ... you can make it up ...

The flexibility and openness of the FT process may appear intimidating, but it was clear that the children felt the model created during workshops was an empowering experience.

This chapter has looked at the workshop stage of FT and has considered key elements of the process including story construction, character development, principles of facilitating the group process and some of the benefits of investing in an FT project. Next we will consider the performance stage of FT.

Chapter 3

The performance

*[The play] showed you what can happen and how you can deal with it
like the audience said ... like it shows you what reality can be like with
some people ... Like if you do get bullied, you don't let it carry on, you
do something about it.*

(Y6 forum theatre participant)

Purpose: To present the play developed in workshops to a group of spect-
actors, providing an opportunity for exploration of the theme and solutions
to the presenting challenges through the use of forum. The process has the
potential to develop the actors' and spect-actors' cognitive, creative and
emotional abilities.

Introduction

The performance in FT consists of two components: presentation of the
play or, alternatively, three or four vignettes, and the forum where spect-
actors have the opportunity to conclude the play in a more desirable way.
This chapter explores both stages, but focuses mainly on the forum.

The play

The weeks spent in the workshops all lead to this moment, the presentation
of the play. The Transition and Empathy projects were both performed in
a community hall next door to the primary school. Thirty minutes before
the play was due to start the actor group were brought into the space. The
children took some time to familiarize themselves with their surroundings
and completed some warm-up activities. They had a little time to run
through their vignette briefly before the spect-actors arrived. There were
children from Reception class upwards, aged 4 to 10. The spect-actors later
became involved with the forum element through discussion, debate, hot-
seating and role reversal. The wider audience – parents, school governors and
representatives from the local authority were there as observers. Teachers
and the head teacher acted as Auxiliary Jokers – or assistant facilitators –
enabling all the spect-actors to participate fully.

The idea of FT was introduced to the spect-actors in the following way:

- We are about to use a special type of theatre called forum theatre.
- We are going to watch a play put together by the Year Six children.

- The play will end with a challenge, or challenges, for one or more of our characters.
- Later you will have the opportunity to help our characters overcome their challenge(s).

The Y6 children took to the stage and performed their play. It maintained a safe distance from worries and anxieties for the spect-actors, but at the same time the spect-actors felt close to the protagonist because they could readily identify with features of the character's situation. This is the paradoxical theory of change in action. In the follow-up focus group, children from the spect-actor group were able to reflect on their initial feelings:

NH: ... which part of it made you feel worried?

Y3SA: When I saw, like, this I was just, like, 'oh how am I going to get by in my new school?' Because it's quite big and it's just, it's like I said, it's three times as big as this school, so it's really big. And, um, I'm not going to have my sister because she is going to be in the infant school and that, and I'm going to be in Year Four, so it's kind of like I'm gonna, I'm not gonna be with her and I'm going to be a bit scared. 'Cos now that I'm in the Juniors I can sort of, like, look through the window and check she's OK, I don't even see her at playtime or in assembly or at lunch ... In my new school we have a different time for lunch, we don't see her at break time, and we don't even see her at assemblies. It's quite scary.

NH: ... what parts of the forum theatre made you feel worried?

[Context: this child chooses to talk about the bullying scene where the protagonist was trying to find his way around his new school with a map when he runs into the antagonist.]

Y3SA: When, when [name of actor] ... was acting out walking along with his [map] ... and he [the antagonist] took away the [map], 'what you don't need that for, it's just a silly old report!' [re-enacts section of play] ... and then threw it in the bin. I'm scared that, I thought that I was going to be, like, bullied ...

NH: OK ... it was the little performances when, when they had a challenge, that made you feel ...

Y3SA: Yeah.

This spect-actor was grounded in his own worries that resonated with the protagonist's challenge. Yet several elements of this spect-actor's story were not reflected in the play, such as issues around siblings or break times. The spect-actor had fed his own thoughts, feelings and experiences into the play. This supports the idea that each one of the spect-actors brings their own context and projects it onto the play.

The play can cause some unease for adults too. Adults often report feeling the heightened anxiety among the spect-actors, paradoxically, not knowing that this is a constructive element to the forum. A play must resonate with the spect-actors so the story feels tangible, relevant and realistic to them as well as provoking them to want to *do* something to help the protagonist.

Boal (1995) describes the play as a mirror where the spect-actors can reflect, a feature highlighted by a child in a particular incident from a different FT project: following the initial play, a child put her hand up and, in reference to some low-level classroom disruption shown, explained that you don't see anything wrong with what you're doing when you're in that place. It's only when someone holds a mirror up to the behaviour that you realize it is an inappropriate way to act. Her reflection encapsulates the paradoxical basis for meaningful change (Biesser, 1970).

The mirror, created by the vignette or play, reflects the issues under investigation. In that reflection small details – behaviour, emotions and thoughts – can be magnified. This allows spect-actors to see the hidden aspects and explore them in greater detail. However, such magnification may temporarily increase the worries for the spect-actors. In a follow-up focus group the children in the spect-actor group were able to articulate how the reflections of realism initially heightened their concerns:

NH: Can you tell me about your experience? What did you think, what did you feel?

Y5SA: Really worried about going up to high school.

NH: You felt worried about going up to high school? OK.

Y5SA: ... worried about going up to high school because, um, my brother goes to Bluebell Academy. He's fourteen now ... and, um, one of these bullies called [him], um, he threw him into a thorn bush. But luckily a police lady's up in Bluebell Academy.

NH: So, it made you feel a little bit worried. Did it make you think or feel anything else?

Y5SA: Um, it made me scared. I felt like I didn't want to go a year higher.

Y3SA: Because it's going to be scarier?

Y5SA: That means you get closer to high school and I'm, like, 'ahh, I don't want to go to high school'.

Negative feelings are usually only a temporary state that are contained by the process. These feelings are important because they provide the catalyst for spect-actors to attempt change. Furthermore, these concerns already exist for these children; they are not new and nor are they induced by the drama. Instead, the emotions are contained and brought to the surface in a safe and effective way by drama. Some psychologists believe that a meaningful art experience should intend to evoke emotion and this is certainly desirable for FT to be effective:

> An art-experience is worth your while only if it leads you to a difficult identification, some possibility in yourself different from what is customary in action.
>
> (Perls et al., 1951/2009: 122)

The initial discussion

After the initial run-through of the play, the Y6 children went to sit at the side of the stage and a short discussion was held with the spect-actors, led by the facilitator. There is no strict formula for such discussions, but good questions to ask are: Where are our characters? What is the setting? Who has the challenge? What is the challenge? What are our central character's thoughts and feelings? Keep the discussions brief, no longer than ten minutes as the momentum created by the play should not be lost.

The purpose of the discussion is to get the spect-actors to think about what they saw happening in the play and allow them safely to place their own thoughts, feelings and experiences onto it. The discussions encourage the spect-actors to identify the protagonist and antagonist, who may be different from what was rehearsed in the workshops. In the case of the Transition Project the spect-actors agreed that the pre-determined protagonist and antagonist were correctly identified.

The re-run and forum

After the discussions, the spect-actors voted on which of the three vignettes they wanted to try to resolve, and chose stories one and two. Story one was about a Y7 child starting in their new secondary school – the protagonist – and facing a Y9 bully – the antagonist. Story two focused on a group of girls who transferred from primary to secondary school together and another Y7 girl with no friends who tried to join the group – seen as the original protagonist. She was rejected by the group leader – originally seen as the antagonist, but later identified as the protagonist. The third story was not used in the forum as we ran out of time. However, the children did have the opportunity to work on the third vignette in school at a later date. Time may constrain the possibilities to work through all of the play or vignettes so it is useful to have a plan of how these unresolved aspects can be explored later.

The spect-actors were told they could shout 'Stop!' as soon as they saw or heard anything that might present a challenge to the protagonist. This was rehearsed with the spect-actors and before the play started by counting to three and asking the children to put their hands up and shout 'Stop!'. The chosen vignette was then run from the start.

The tools of forum

The children shouted 'Stop!', as rehearsed, and the Auxiliary Jokers, made up of teaching staff, were among the spect-actors to support their participation. Once the spect-actor stopped the action, the facilitator moved in. First, I wanted to know why the spect-actor had stopped the action: what was it about the action that was particularly important? In a very short discussion I asked questions such as:

- What made you shout 'Stop!'?
- What is the challenge? Who has the challenge? Who is the challenger?
- Do the other spect-actors with their hands up agree with these views?
- What might be an alternative explanation to what we have seen?

This is not an exhaustive list and not all these questions need to be asked each time a spect-actor stops the action. However, they indicate how the spect-actors are encouraged to debate, question and consider alternative perspectives. Such questioning may lead to competing views on what needs to happen next. In these cases the group may take a vote, or if time allows it may be possible to see both ideas played out. After the discussion and debate, several other tools were used to engage the spect-actors further, as follows:

- **Hot-seating**: one actor is chosen to sit in a chair and answer questions from the spect-actors while in character. This helped clarify the motivation and background of the character in question.
- **Role reversal**: the spect-actors take the place of the protagonist and attempt to overcome the challenge with their own ideas.

- **Introduce new characters**: one spect-actor attempts change by calling on another spect-actor to help them out in the role of a new character. An extension to this is where a spect-actor intervenes while a character is being hot-seated and becomes the character's unconscious. The spect-actor stands next to the hot seat and while the actor is responding to questions the spect-actor shouts out alternative motivations. Here is an example, where a spect-actor from the audience (SAA) is hot-seating the antagonist (Y6A) and another spect-actor (SA(A)) is speaking as the antagonist's unconscious:

  - **SAA**: Why are you being so mean?
  - **Y6A**: I'm not being mean, I'm trying to help him.
  - **SA(A)**: I'm jealous of his popularity, I used to be the popular one around here. Why shouldn't I give him a hard time?

The spect-actors can choose to believe what the actor is saying or the spect-actor's alternative view, and this can often split opinion and create debate among the spect-actors.

- **Offer suggestions**: the spect-actors suggest possible alternatives to the actor who is playing the protagonist. This is useful when children are not confident about speaking up or when a spect-actor who is already in role gets stuck.

It is important that the actor group has some experience of these tools during the workshops and develop appropriate skills in improvisation and the FT game. Despite anticipating these issues in the workshops, in FT anything can happen. Here the actor group reflect on their experience during the forum part of the performance and the challenges this posed:

> NH: ... is there anything about the experience of doing a forum theatre performance that you particularly remember thinking or feeling?

> Y6A(3): Confused.

> NH: Confused. OK, can you tell me a little bit more about ...

> Y6A(3): When [a spect-actor] came up and gave me really hard, eh, erm, kind of scene to ... he like moved out the way and I had to think of something really quick which would go with what he did.

In order to support these challenges I use the huddle. This technique is used whenever a spect-actor swaps roles with the protagonist. Here is a quick reminder of the huddle's purpose:

- to provide clarity to the actor about what the spect-actor is suggesting
- to provide a reminder that the actor's response should be realistic but not too easy for the spect-actor
- to provide a reminder of the character's motivations
- to provide a reminder that there is no single right way of reacting – the important point is to enjoy the play and have fun.

The children in the actor group were able to respond remarkably well and this did not go unnoticed by their teachers:

> NH: ... can you generally just tell me about your experiences of the forum theatre performance on Monday.
>
> HT: I was really impressed by just how capable ... they were. I was quite shocked by some of the transformations. [laughs]
>
> KS2CT: It was very realistic.
>
> HT: So I thought, you know, I thought they were ... really convincing. I think that helped, I think they convinced their audience, the little audience as opposed to the adult audience. I think they convinced their little audience that they, I think they forgot who they were, which is a huge compliment to them.

A combination of high quality workshops and tried-and-tested techniques used throughout the forum led to the children being very able in their responses. As the head teacher remarked here, the actor group created scenes and characters that were believable. The children took on their characters with confidence, leading to a play that successfully sustained a make-believe world for the spect-actors.

Psychology in action

The observer

Not all spect-actors took part by engaging in active elements of the forum such as role swapping or discussion. But nor were they passive as their observation was, in itself, an action:

> A spectator means to be a participant, intervening; here to be a spectator means to prepare oneself for action, and preparing oneself is already in itself an action.
>
> (Boal, 1995: 72)

Ideally, as many of the spect-actors as possible will pose questions and swap roles. However if a large number of observers choose to remain, this does not mean a project has been unsuccessful. In the Transition and Empathy projects there were a number of observers among the spect-actor group. Here, the actor group reflects on the role of the observers, after the performance:

> **Y6A(1):** Um, you could act it out and then ... you could like, not copy it but, like, ...
>
> **Y6A(3):** Yeah, copy it.
>
> **Y6A(1):** Play it out. Yeah, like kind of copy it ...
>
> **Y6A(3):** When it happened you can say 'oh' and you just get on with it like you did with the play and, but not like the bad way, but like the good way that people have, um, given ideas and helped you with it.

This discussion of how the observers could imitate solutions they had seen captures the essence of SLT (Bandura *et al.*, 1963) as a very powerful form of learning. In SLT one observes behaviour that leads to imitation in the real world when faced with similar situations.

Rehearsal and embodied play

The rehearsal aspect of the forum is important as it allows different solutions to be tried out by spect-actors through a process called embodied play, whereby children act on, and within, their world, for instance by getting up and swapping roles. Embodied play can help stimulate cognitive processes such as thinking, reasoning and information-processing; this is known as embodied cognition (Shapiro, 2011).

Rehearsal is a repeated activity in FT. Children are able, through rehearsal, to develop different ways of seeing their world (Kelly, 1963). When used over time, this approach can support them to feel more optimistic and empowered to overcome their own real-life challenges. While it is not the intentional application of FT to therapeutically alter emotional or behavioural responses (as explained in Chapter 2), the process has the inherent potential to empower children and help them grow in confidence.

In the Transition Project, several spect-actors tried out their ideas to help the protagonist overcome their challenge. During the forum of story one, a spect-actor (SAA) offered an idea to help out the protagonist – a new Y7 child:

> **SAA:** I think ... corridors are quite wide and he could ... well he's [the antagonist] sort of acting like he wants everyone to feel like they've done something bad and, um, he could have just, um, walked on, at the edge. And, [spect-actor in protagonist role] could have, um, been a little bit nicer to [the antagonist] and [the antagonist] might have been nicer back.

> **F:** OK, so at the end of this scene it could have ended on something negative but [the protagonist] could have been a bit nicer and that might have changed it, you think? OK, do you want to come up and give it a go?

Based on her observations, this spect-actor identified the challenge and why it might exist – the antagonist is not very nice, but the protagonist might be perceived as confrontational too. The spect-actor then generated an idea about what might help – that the protagonist could be nicer to the antagonist. The new spect-actor (SA(10)) replaced her peer – another spect-actor playing the protagonist – and tried out her new idea to be nicer toward the antagonist (Y6A(3)). The process of rehearsal to overcome the challenge began:

> **Y6A(3):** What are you doing with that? Would you rather be lost or would you rather be bullied?

> **SA(10):** Actually, I'm looking for somebody to actually take me around the school.

> **Y6A(3):** Go ask one of the Year Sevens. [actor walks off stage past the spect-actor]

At this point many spect-actors wanted to take the place of the antagonist, because the antagonist remained hostile even though the protagonist changed their approach. But, it's important that spect-actors only rehearse the role of the protagonist because simply changing the antagonist's behaviour is not only too simple but also unrealistic. Imagine a scene where a spect-actor takes the role of the Y9 bully in this story and makes him more flexible and friendly toward our protagonist: the challenge has been removed and the FT game ends, but the spect-actors are unlikely to gain much from the experience.

We cannot change the behaviour of others directly, but we may change our own behaviour in a way that affects that of others. FT provides a space in which to rehearse for real life, so simulating reality is important. Spect-actors continued to feel that although suggestions had helped move closer to a desirable resolution, there was room to help the protagonist further. Another spect-actor stopped the action, this time suggesting that he be more assertive with the Y9 pupil:

Y6A(3): What are you doing with that?

SA(7): How would you like it if somebody did it to you? [antagonist looks a little shocked] How, how would you like it if somebody did it to you?

Y6A(3): Do what?

SA(7): [Bully a] Year Seven!

Y6A(3): I was just trying to look out for ya.

SA(7): So …

Y6A(3): Would you rather be lost or would you rather be bullied?

SA(7): Actually … I was finding where I was going …

This assertive intervention from the spect-actor altered the course of the play yet again. This time we started to see another possible motivation from the antagonist – where the antagonist was initially perceived as being aggressive and intimidating, it began to emerge that the motivation behind these actions might have been kinder. During the hot-seating of the antagonist, the spect-actors were keen to know why he was bullying the protagonist. The antagonist explained that he was not bullying, but trying to help the protagonist ease into secondary school. He went on to say that he was bullied in Y7 and was now trying to help his new school mates to settle. Whether true or an improvised excuse, our spect-actors remained sceptical.

The scene was started again from where our protagonist became more assertive. However, the spect-actors were able to identify that the solution could create a circular conflict rather than a sustainable resolution, so it was not too long before another spect-actor was compelled to swap roles with the protagonist:

F: OK, there's a stop, there's a stop.

SAA: Instead of arguing I'd just walk away from him.

F: OK, let's give it a go. [the spect-actors swap over]

Y6A(3): What are you doing with that? Would you rather be lost or would you rather be bullied?

SA(8): OK, alright [the spect-actor walks past actor] I was just [inaudible words] teacher.

This collective rehearsal extends the original ideas proposed by Kelly (1963) by allowing different spect-actors to strengthen solutions through collaboration. In a follow-up discussion with spect-actors after the Transition Project, the idea of rehearsal was considered to be one of the most helpful aspects of FT:

NH: How do you think [FT] could be useful?

Y4SA: When you're moving up, when you're mov ... doing something it could be very useful 'cos you'd know all the problems that could happen and stuff like that, you know how to solve it and ... then it'll be fine.

The process of rehearsal can instil confidence in the spect-actors to try to overcome challenges in reality. Whether this is too ambitious is explored in Chapter 4. However, it is proven that the ability to show, rather than express answers verbally, can be empowering. Here, a Reception child demonstrates his response toward an antagonist through the idea of embodied play:

Y6A(3): What are you doing, you're in the middle of the corridor!

SA(5): [throws hands in air] Uh. [moves to one side out of the way of actor 3]

AF: Have you moved to one side [name of spect-actor] to let him pass? You moved to one side.

SA(5): Yeah.

AF: Do you want to say something to [actor 3]?

SA(5): [points and says something very softly to actor 3 – inaudible].

SA(5): [moves around actor 2 and walks off the other side of the stage].

Here we see how the actor (Y6A(3)) in this segment attempts to stick with the original model – to intimidate the protagonist – and the spect-actor (SA(5)) simply side-steps the actor and walks away, far from the counter-conflict offered by some other spect-actors. This 4-year-old spect-actor is able to show his response to the antagonist in a manner that leaves the actor speechless and clearly defuses the conflict. And the process of swapping roles and rehearsing solutions is not limited to finding desirable outcomes; there are other notable benefits of embodied play such as the stimulation of cognitive processes. One of these is meta-cognition – that is, thinking about our own thinking.

In this example, the spect-actors are working through story two: Rebecca is the antagonist, as the leader of a small group of girls who moved to secondary school together. Phoebe has moved to the same secondary school but there is no one else from her previous school and she was our protagonist at this stage. Another character, Lucy, is a friend of Rebecca, who wants to reach out to Phoebe. In this example, a spect-actor is already in role as Phoebe (SA(1)) and another spect-actor (SAA) is offering some views from the audience. Encouraged by the facilitator the spect-actors demonstrate their meta-cognitive skills:

SAA: When she was, um, Rebecca, um, when she was, stomping, it was like she was trying to, um, boss Phoebe around.

F: Yeah, so it could be some of that going on ... so what do we, what do we think Phoebe ... should do now?

SA(1): ... she should stand up ... she's my friend, come on, eh I could stand up and say 'she's my friend too'.

F: OK, alright, let's see how Phoebe does. Let's see how she does. OK ...

Y6A(6): Lucy, I told you to leave her alone. Come on!

SA(1): [standing up] Hey! She's my friend too you know [crosses arms]. She's not just yours.

Y6A(6): You only started today.

SA(1): And?

Y6A(6): You can't just be friends after about one hour.

SA(1): [turns to Lucy] Lucy, are you my friend?

Y6A(5): Um, well, I guess I'm kind of friends with both of you.

SA(1): See?

Y6A(6): Arrgh! [storms off stage]

In this scenario spect-actors offer their observations, while the facilitator challenges the participant to think further about their response: 'What do you think Phoebe should do now?' The spect-actor, in role as Phoebe, considers and responds in the way he thinks would reach a more desirable outcome. It is plausible to assume he is thinking from his character's perspective when finding his response. However, the child knows very little about the protagonist at this stage other than the situation as it is presented within the play. Furthermore, the spect-actor empathizes with how the protagonist feels and thinks by drawing on his own experiences, as the protagonist's history is not revealed – and even if it were, the experience would belong to the character, not the child. Thus, through embodied play the child is actually encouraged to think about his own thinking as if he were in the position of the character, rather than being the character *per se*. Two examples of meta-cognition can be seen in this forum extract. The first is known as meta-cognitive control – where a spect-actor decides when to stop the action and change events based on what they have seen in the play. The second is known as meta-cognitive monitoring – where the child makes a judgement about a possible solution and when the optimal outcome has been achieved (Dunlosky and Metcalfe, 2009). In a follow-up discussion, teaching staff identified how FT can enhance children's thinking skills:

> HT: [FT is] a tool for thinking something through even if [the children] don't end up taking control of it, at least they'll, you know ... instead of us standing at the front and saying right ... with a partner ... think about how you'll feel in Year Seven and talk about it for 20 minutes, and then feed back to everybody. You can get something out of that, but it can be very hit-and-miss, whereas [in the FT] they're almost being forced to respond by what was being thrown at them and to ... think through what was going on.

Problem-solving

FT can also support the development of children's problem-solving repertoires. A problem-solving repertoire is built on the skills, tools and ideas one has to solve problems or challenges. The more of these skills children have, the more confident they feel at solving real-life problems.

Problem-solving skills in FT are developed through:

- creating a realistic play (by providing a tangible context in which a problem may occur)
- supporting realistic improvisations from the actor group (encouraging responses that could, potentially, be re-created in real-life, as opposed to abstract ideas)
- appropriate and sensitive challenging from the facilitator to spect-actors (by encouraging the children to reflect on their suggestions and whether they feel these ideas are too simplistic or likely to be inadequate)
- eliciting a variety of ideas and not settling for simple solutions (remember, our starting points are fixed, so simple suggestions such as 'tell the teacher about the bullying' is likely to have already been incorporated into the play. While simplicity can be effective, we want to extend the children's ideas, not re-invent the whccl!)
- allowing spect-actors to swap roles with the protagonist (this is the central idea of embodied cognition; by encouraging children to swap roles with the protagonist only – at least initially – they are afforded the opportunity to actively rehearse and play in a safe space. So instead of being cognitive about what they might do, they can actually try it out).

This last point is particularly important. This extract, taken from a recording of the forum session, shows how a spect-actor makes an attempt to change the antagonist (Rebecca):

> F: ... OK [spect-actor] what do you think?
>
> SAA: Well, she [Rebecca] shouldn't start questioning Phoebe. She shouldn't, like, shout at her. She should have said ... 'Hello Phoebe'.
>
> F: ... what do you think we can do with, how do you think Phoebe could respond?

The spect-actor is sensitively refocused on the protagonist, Phoebe, because changing the antagonist is unlikely to be a realistic solution in real life. If we had accepted this spect-actor's idea, the FT game would have been over as the challenge would have been removed – Rebecca would have not presented Phoebe with a challenge. The facilitator uses a range of questions to highlight assumptions and tackle simplification, including:

- How do we know ...?
- What if ...?
- But [name of character] did/said ...
- Do you think [scenario/outcome/solution] would happen/work in real life?
- What don't we know?
- What isn't being said?

The forum element works in a similar way to De Bono's artificial mechanical problem (1970: 245). In story one our protagonist experienced bullying, and some obvious solutions, such as ignoring and walking away, had already been exhausted. The protagonist could not remove himself from the setting and would always see the antagonist at break times. This meant spect-actors had to overcome the challenge within restricted starting points. Spect-actors are made aware of these restrictions through the original play, hot-seating, discussion and debate. The spect-actors are then forced to consider creative ideas that go beyond the obvious. In the process, problem-solving repertoires can be extended for use in the real world (De Bono, 1970). In this next extract, Rebecca, our antagonist from story two, is in the hot seat. Notice how our antagonist remains defended, thus restricting where the spect-actors are able to make suggestions to overcome the challenge:

SAA: When [Rebecca] says 'I've got loads of friends', [Phoebe] should have said 'Where are they? Where are they?'

F: ... do we know all about these characters? Do we need to ask them anything, do we need to ask these characters any questions?

[Actor in character as Rebecca sits in the 'hot seat']

SAA: Why are you snappy in the first place?

Y6A(6): Because I'm the top dog ...

SAA: How many friends do you actually have?

Y6A(6): Lots, they're just sick.

F: What, they're just sick? What off school sick?

Y6A(6): Yeah.

SAA: Why do you ... want to be like this?

Y6A(6): Because I just want to.

SAA: Couldn't you do with some more friends?

Y6A(6): The table's already full where we all sit.

SAA: Um, do you think you should be more nice to [Phoebe]?

Y6A(6): No. She'll probably just steal my friends.

SAA: ... surely all of your friends apart from two, can't be sick. And I think you're hiding a little secret.

Y6A(6): They've got swine flu. [spect-actors laugh]

SAA: So why haven't you got swine flu?

Y6A(6): Because they haven't been coming to school.

F: What do you think the secret is? [lots of hands go up]

SAA: I think she's trying to hide something ... if they don't go to school, and they don't come to you [inaudible word] catch it. So, they don't come to you, why don't you just have another friend ...?

Y6A(6): I got a letter from them last week and it said that they were getting better and they were coming back to school next week.

These responses limit the possible solutions for spect-actors. However, through the hot-seating process spect-actors begin to uncover subtle motivations of the antagonist that enable creative questioning and solutions. The following extract shows how creative ideas need not be extravagant; here, spect-actors reflect on how effectively Phoebe uses silence:

SAA: I thought it was good how after saying her favourite subject she left a space of silence. Literally making her, making Rebecca say something.

F: So you, you thought the silence was good?

SAA: Yeah.

F: OK, good. What do you think she was trying to tell her by leaving that space of silence?

SAA: Um, trying ... to make her be nice, trying to see what she likes ...

Problem-solving in the moment can be extremely demanding. FT supports children by giving them an opportunity to observe, reflect and rehearse solutions to real concerns. Over time these opportunities can help develop problem-solving repertoires that can be drawn-on in the moment.

Parallel thinking (De Bono, 1986) is another important aspect of the forum. Here all spect-actors and other audience members, regardless of which character they are drawn to, are encouraged to think about resolving the same challenge. The spect-actors and the broader audience are made up of: those who face, or might face, the challenges presented; those who represent, or are perceived to be, the challengers; and those who can support the challenged in overcoming the barriers they might face.

In story three of the Transition Project the two characters were challenged by the appeals system, but also by family and friends who inflated the status of the schools. These multiple challenges heightened the conflict between the two friends. Having key stakeholders such as parents, friends, teachers and representatives from the local authority attending the performance day meant the most relevant people could join together to consider the issue and resolve the challenge. Everyone was looking at the same problem, bringing their own views to the play and working together to find a solution.

The development of cognitive skills such as creative thinking, reasoning and problem-solving was highly regarded by the teaching staff. Following the performance day, the head teacher remarked on FT's ability to support these cognitive skills and how valuable the experience had been:

> HT: Well, I think if you take the ... idea that [professionals are] working with us to develop children's thinking then I think [FT is] entirely legitimate. Just what we asked you to do really – motivation, thinking, taking, you know, independent thought, taking control of all those things ...

Finding solutions

FT brings children's concerns around the theme to the surface safely. Those in the actor group are encouraged to externalize their concerns, and spect-actors use the safe space, which has been created by the stories and characters, to find solutions. Simultaneous with the externalization process, the actors and spect-actors recognize their own concerns around the theme – in this case transition. This process is known as the paradoxical theory of change, as described earlier.

The children are next encouraged to imagine a world where the challenge has been removed. Boal calls this the oneiric dimension (Boal,

1995: 22); where the child is encouraged to dream without limitation. Using the tools of forum, children can play, reflect, rehearse and consider complex social and emotional elements of the challenges. They are also given the tools to find realistic and sustainable solutions. In a follow-up discussion with a group of spect-actors, one child reflected on how the play made the worries more present – paradoxical change; but by the end she felt much more confident about her inevitable transition:

> **Y5SA:** ... it would be very worrying when, um, I go to high school and, um, you know about on the Monday, the bullying? It just gave me an idea because, um, you know they seemed like OK with being bullied and saying and stop, well forget about that do you wanna be friends? And, um, you could say that to, um, if someone was bullying you at your new school or, um, your different school that you're about to move in, like high school. Um, you could just go, if someone's about to start bullying you, and you could just tell, and you can go 'hey do you wanna be friends?' and they'll be like 'I weren't expecting that.'

> **NH:** It was ... certainly an interesting idea. So it gave you ... some ideas? How did that make you feel?

> **Y5SA:** It made me feel more comfortable for moving up to high school and in a different year if new people come in.

The spect-actors were not the only ones to benefit from this solution-focused approach; the actor group also reported on the usefulness of the solutions offered. Here the group discuss their thoughts after the performance day:

> **Y6A(3):** Yeah, so it's like, eh, it's like someone trying to help someone, what kind of a lot of people ... a whole audience trying to help someone.

> **NH:** Right ... was that useful or un-useful for you? 'Cos you're going to Year Seven.

> **Y6A(1):** Um, it was really useful I felt.

> **Y6A(2):** Yeah.

Finding solutions can be extended further by asking the spect-actors 'miracle questions' (De Shazer and Dolan, 2007: 37). A typical miracle question would be: 'Suppose we had a magic wand and all the challenges we see here were resolved:

- What would we notice?
- What would be different?
- What would the people or systems be doing differently?
- What would be the first step toward that miracle situation?'

A key outcome of FT is to empower children to see that their ideas have created a significant change for the protagonist. In other words FT ends with an idea of how life can be:

> Inviting [children] to talk about their past successes, their strengths, and where they want to be when they have an ideal outcome empowers them to create their own positive self-fulfilling prophecies.
>
> (Selekman, 1997: 72)

During a follow-up discussion this Y5 child observes how having children as actors is an important part of making the scenario feel realistic and therefore the solutions more tangible:

> **Y5SA:** And the other children that are watching it, um, would get the idea of children actually doing it. And it actually happening to them instead of adults.

Here the child is emphasizing a key difference between the FT approach used with children as actors (which typically feels very real to the children taking part) and other forms of theatre in which children's experiences are interpreted by adult actors (which may be more difficult for the children to engage with on a personal level).

Returning to the Transition Project, as we got to the end of the allotted FT time, the spect-actors were given the chance to see some of their solutions worked into a final play. Here are the steps we went through before showing a final play with the incorporated solutions:

- Key solutions for each vignette were identified by the facilitator.
- These options were presented to the spect-actors.
- A quick vote was taken to decide which solutions would be used in the final play.
- The facilitator took notes.
- The facilitator convened a huddle with the actor group.
- The steps to the revised solution-focused model were confirmed.
- The final play, including solutions, was run.

Story one was revised to end in a more desirable way following the forum process:

> **Y6A(3):** What are you doing with that? Would you rather be lost or would you rather be bullied?
>
> **SA(11):** Well, to actually be honest I was actually looking for somebody to take me around the school. I'm quite lost.
>
> **Y6A(3):** Well, yeah, I can probably help you. If you're not bugging me. Just follow me and don't do anything silly. [audience laugh]
>
> **F:** OK ... what do you think? What d'ya think, yeah?
>
> **SAA:** Um, at least that they [actor 3] ... sort of said it like he doesn't want to do it, but he'll do it.
>
> **F:** Right.
>
> **SAA:** But, on the other hand, the fact that they're, um, it's time for them to, eh, sort of talk to each other and get along better.

No magical solution was found to story one; but life, too, is imperfect. Compromise is almost always inevitable which is a valuable discussion to be had within the FT – the process is a catalyst for change, not an end-result. Generally, the children felt confident to use their new skills and utilize their own strengths in the real world. However, while many of the children will feel that their concerns have been resolved by the forum, some may not. As this Y3 child explained, FT feels very real and can therefore help children build their confidence in solving life's challenges. However, just as in real life, while some challenges may be entirely resolved, the perfect solution might not always be possible and residual doubts may remain:

> **Y3SA:** ... forum theatre sort of like explaining how it was going to be when you're, like, growing up. But you can, you can, you know you can, sort it out. But you're not always a hundred per cent ...

This outcome is inevitable for some; although FT offers many opportunities, it cannot provide a rehearsal for every eventuality. And in some ways, reflecting the imperfection of real life is desirable.

In a follow-up discussion with teaching staff, there was agreement that FT could offer a notable platform for the children to take control of their own learning:

KS2CT: It got more responses from a wider variety of children than that session in the classroom would get. So, a much broader coverage isn't it?

HT: Yeah and I think as well what became fascinating for us and I think also for the older children was the way that your little lot were responding [addresses KS1 teacher]. 'Cos, I suspect the Juniors sort of went in with a bit of an inkling as to what was going to happen, because getting some feedback from the Year Sixes was inevitable. But I think they sort of [thought] 'oh, well', you know 'they're just here to make up the numbers' ... it was very, you know, there was a lot of feedback from the younger ones. And confident feedback as well ...

There's something about empathy

The Transition Project raised two key questions in the area of emotional development: What role could FT play in developing empathy? And is using FT in this way desirable? To explore these areas further a second, much smaller, study was undertaken, referred to here as the Empathy Project.

Empathy is often seen as a desirable quality, so it may surprise many to know that Boal heavily critiqued empathy:

Empathy must be understood as the terrible weapon it really is. Empathy is the most dangerous weapon in the entire arsenal of the theatre and related arts (movies and TV).

(Boal, 1979: 93)

We have already seen that developing empathy is inherent to FT; Babbage (2004) even argued that FT relied on empathy as spect-actors identify with each character. In addition, workshop activities such as Yeti Language, and forum tools such as swapping roles, specifically aim to promote empathy:

this device [role reversal] may seem artificial, but it develops a surprising amount of reality and at times can become just as real.

(Rogers, 1951: 469)

Boal's concern was that the antagonist may have likeable qualities that can lead to spect-actors empathizing with, and perhaps justifying, the antagonist's actions (Boal, 1979). However, Boal's position assumes that empathy operates in isolation of the spect-actors' history or experiences. It is also possible that Boal's concerns are more about imitation than empathy: that spect-actors might copy the behaviour of antagonists rather than justify the antagonists' cause. In fact, psychologists have known for some time that empathy is important in the negation of aggressive behaviour (Van Evra, 1990).

The Empathy Project focused on one short play. Our antagonist was Mary, the school bully, and the protagonist was Patrick, the object of Mary's aggression. Later it was discovered that Mary had problems at home that affected her behaviour in school. The play ended with Patrick's brothers bullying Mary in a revenge attack. The play was developed and the forum took place in the same way as the Transition Project but over a much shorter time. The project showed something quite intriguing about the subject matter: empathy was not the disaster Boal made out, but neither was it as desirable as educators and psychologists might think, especially if appropriate management is lacking.

Following the FT, a group of children from both the actor and spect-actor groups were invited to share their views about the play. In this extract, the children discuss their feelings toward bullying. What is remarkable is how the children begin to justify the bullying behaviour of Patrick's brothers:

NH: ... what do you think about bullying?

Y4: Um, I think you'll hurt them from the inside because it's not very nice bullying people and then if someone bullies those who've been bullying other people they would see how it feels like to be bullied.

Y5(1): ... you know that Mary was bullying then, yeah ... um, maybe they could like, um, 'cos it wasn't nice, maybe, Mary could [have a taste of] her own medicine ...

NH: Mary could ...?

Y5(1): Mary could, like, have her own medicine because she's been bullying people ... and she's been bullied back.

NH: Did you think it was OK for Mary to be bullied because she was bullying someone else?

Y5(2): Yes. I thought it was OK.

Y5(1): I think yes and no.

Overall, the children felt it was reasonable for Mary to be bullied, in light of her behaviour toward Patrick. This was despite Mary sharing information about her difficult home life. Although the children empathized with her, her difficulties at home were not seen as justifying her behaviour toward Patrick. However, the children seemed to empathize enough with Patrick's predicament, as the underdog perhaps, and this led to Patrick's brothers' retaliation being accepted as legitimate. Therefore, empathy and the children's acceptance of a counter-productive resolution appear to be due to a complex combination of empathy for the character, contextual circumstances of the story and personal experiences, as this extract from the children's discussion shows:

> Y5(2): ... sometimes I feel a bit lost because, well, my dad says, um, if someone, like, hits you, you hit them back and go and tell the teacher and then when I have done it, like in my old school, my mum's been saying 'no, no, no, you don't hit 'em' and my dad's been saying 'hit 'em' ...
>
> NH: ... how does that make you feel?
>
> Y5(2): Eh, puzzled.
>
> NH: OK. [Pause] A little like Mary perhaps? ... In that she was puzzled.
>
> Y6: My brother does that, my brother says, 'ah if, if they're really mean to ya, just [inaudible word] 'em' and my dad's like 'no don't' and 'you just walk away', and I'm, like, 'what am I supposed to do?!'
>
> Y5(1): Which choice d'you make?
>
> Y6: Yeah.
>
> NH: And what do you think you would do?
>
> Y6: Um ...
>
> Y5: ... walk away if it was a really seri- ... a really tough guy.

External influences from family members are accepted as justification for retaliation. In Patrick's case, that was his brothers' response to Mary. It is unsurprising that children feel confused when they receive conflicting messages about how to manage the challenges they face. Social influences appear more dominant than empathy when they consider how to challenge the antagonist.

Qualitative differences between the two projects, such as shorter workshops, may have reduced the opportunity to explore the children's confusion and their readiness to use their empathy for Patrick counter-productively, by bullying Mary. Nevertheless, the Empathy Project showed that while empathy is essential to FT, it requires careful management. Through the FT process, the children's confusion – which might otherwise remain latent – can be brought to the surface. This extract from discussions with children in the Transition Project – which lasted several weeks – shows empathy as being managed and valued as a constructive element of FT:

> NH: ... how do you think that forum theatre might be helpful?
>
> Y6A(3): To ... not let yourself be too careless. And like, um, trying not to upset people so you're getting yourself into ... deeper trouble. So, like, if like, I was the bully, like try and be a bit nicer and try and [pause] yeah, try and be a bit positive.

The children from the Transition Project were notably in favour of role reversal as a way of developing empathy. In this extract, children from the actor group explained that empathizing with the antagonists was very helpful:

> Y6A(3): I enjoyed, um, doing the workshops and the actual play, 'cos it made me put, like, in the view of a bully and what they have to do to keep their personality ...
>
> NH: Right. Can you tell me a bit more about that?
>
> Y6A(3): ... and reputation. Like if there's someone who's really nasty and ... like, trying to be cool ... they have to do the thing that I did, like kind of, um, eh, be like nasty and ... show off to their friends ...
>
> NH: So that helped you see things from ...
>
> Y6A(3): Their point of view.

This actor explains how role reversal was helpful in empathizing with children who might bully. Earlier, the same child also noted that empathizing allowed him to take care not to be 'too careless' toward others.

The benefits of using FT to develop empathy are not conclusively supported. On the one hand there is a risk that children may empathize with a counter-oppressive solution such as bullying the bully. This risk appears to increase when workshops are run over a short period of time, such as a day or two. Empathy requires consideration through reflection and discussion, to take account of the participant's contextual issues, cultural beliefs, social norms and personal experiences. To this extent, empathy alone is unlikely to create counter-oppressive responses and, if anything, empathy is more likely to negate such responses when managed effectively. As this teacher from the Transition Project observed:

> **KS2CT:** It helps you to understand different points of view on the same behaviour doesn't it? It's a much broader picture of a situation.

FT does offer concrete scenarios that can focus on telemicroscopic social behaviours. The motivations behind one's actions can be illuminated for closer inspection, through which empathy can be managed and perhaps taught, using the child's own experiences as a basis.

However, as we have seen, FT can be an emotionally demanding task, especially for those children who have participated as actors and active spect-actors. Next, we will consider how emotional responses can be managed and supported through de-role and aftercare activities.

Chapter 4

De-role and aftercare

*I really liked it when we could make all those things up. We could
decide what we want[ed] to do ... we weren't elected to be something,
we could say anything we liked ... I wasn't elected to be the person that
I was created into and ... it was quite good actually ... it lets you be
more creative.*

(Y6 forum theatre participant)

Purpose: De-role aims to ensure children are detached from their characters
once the FT performance ends and re-connected to their real life in a safe
and contained way. Aftercare ensures that any residual concerns not resolved
in the FT process can be picked up and managed promptly, efficiently
and safely.

Introduction
There are important safety processes that need to be built into any FT
project. Some are inherent to the process, such as externalization. Others
are essential components to be taken into account and built-in early on in
the project – specifically, de-role and aftercare.

De-role
Once a child has taken on a role it is important that they are also enabled to
leave that role behind. Games and activities can be used that are specifically
designed to allow the child to reconnect with their real-life thoughts,
emotions and physicality. De-role describes the process of the child leaving
behind the fictional character, story, context and all that comes with the
make-believe world, and returning to reality. De-role should take place
throughout the FT project, most notably after each workshop with the actor
group and after the FT performance session – the play and forum – and
should be applied to all the actors and spect-actors who took on roles. It
is essential to have a scheduled time for de-role to take place after each
workshop and the performance session – this is a non-negotiable priority.

Starting with the end
Preparation for de-role starts right at the beginning of the project. The first
consideration is space – it should be big enough to have a defined off- and
on-stage section. In a large room, one end of the space will be where all the
character and story development takes place – that is, on-stage. The other

end of the room can be used for de-role – off-stage. The venue used in the Transition and Empathy projects was a community hall next door to the primary school. This was helpful because the children had to physically move out of their classroom and cross the playground to reach it. However, space in most settings will be at a premium, and access to a completely separate building is unusual. Some creative thinking may identify another space such as: an unused classroom, intervention room/space, adjacent children's centre, charity or community building, a music/drama/arts room, an assembly hall, a disused office, a local theatre space or even a playground – weather permitting.

Symbolizing change

Drama is unique in providing virtually endless possibilities for symbolizing change through introducing or removing items around a room or on a person. Devices include, for example: using props and sticky labels for character names and costumes (simple items work best such as hats, glasses or jackets) or using objects in the space such as chairs that can be moved around to denote a change of scene or on/off stage. For example, you may have been working in a space that is large enough to split in two: a performance area and a non-performance area. The performance area is where the children are in costume or wear their character's name badge; by removing costume or name tags and walking over to the non-performing area, change is symbolized.

Circle of questioning

The children stand in a circle and the facilitator goes around the circle in no particular order, addressing a child by name and asking how they think they differ from their character. Other children in the circle can comment on how they think their peer is different from the character. The aim is to draw out positive differences; this is especially important for children who have played the antagonist. If a participant accidently refers to a child by their character name, the facilitator promptly says the child's real name, explicitly distinguishing them from their character.

Right to reply

Each child gets themselves a chair and lines it up with others in a round. Each child stands behind their chair and follows this sequence until they have all taken their turn:

- The child moves around to the front of their chair.
- The child removes the sticky label with their character's name on it and places it on the chair.

- The facilitator asks what, if anything, the child would like to say to their character in parting, such as offering some advice or comment or just saying goodbye.
- Once the children have said everything they want to, they walk across to the other side of the room – off-stage. An alternative is to just symbolize the change by taking off their character's name badge, for example, rather than leaving the circle.
- Once the child moves across the space and off-stage, only their real name can be used. The facilitator can reinforce this by using their real name when acknowledging the child's participation: 'Thank you John'.

This activity is relatively straightforward with the actor group, but when spect-actors are involved it is likely that more than one child will have played any given character. In this instance the actor and the spect-actor are teamed up and go through the process together.

The projective chair

As a variation on the Right to Reply activity, here the children are invited to stand opposite an empty chair and imagine their character is sitting there, while they make a closing statement to them. Typical responses would include saying goodbye or giving advice to them, for example encouraging them to be good or telling them 'I didn't like it when you bullied, that's not nice'. The child should be given this space and time to separate in whatever way they wish. The process aims to clear the child's mind of their thoughts and feelings toward their character and reinforce distance. Two of the children in the Transition Project had fallen out over school placement allocation because only one had received their preferred place, but both were keen to use the sentiment of their situation, such as the emotions they felt, in their characters. These children were particularly aware of their decision to incorporate their real emotions – something they and their peers had brought to the space rather than a reflection made by the facilitator. The projective chair technique offered them an opportunity to indirectly reflect on the situation and find closure on their negative feelings over the issue.

Group evaluation

Evaluation of the workshop offers the opportunity to find out what is, and is not, working well for the children. Ideally the feedback and reflections shared should be only those of the participants, not those of the facilitator (although the facilitator may occasionally need to intervene if the group process gets stuck or goes off-task). Evaluation allows for the facilitator to notice issues early and make adjustments, and gives the group the space to reflect on learning points, thoughts and feelings.

Inviting a colleague into the workshop so they can observe and feed their thoughts back to the group afterwards generally proves extremely useful. Another form of group evaluation also uses an empty chair approach in a different way:

- The children stand in a circle with an empty chair placed in the centre. This provides a tangible focus for them. They are asked to imagine that the workshop is a fictional character sitting in the chair.
- They are then asked collectively to consider the following questions:

  o What kind of character would we describe the workshop as?
  o What compliment would we pay this character?
  o Does the character have a name?
  o What piece of advice would we give this character?
  o What is this character good at?
  o What does this character need to work on?
  o What might the character say to everyone who has taken part?
  o How might the character think and feel: at the start? At the end?

This is not an exhaustive list of questions – so be creative. The idea is that children will project their thoughts about the workshop onto an empty chair, so giving the facilitators clues about how the process was experienced by each child and offering the children a feeling of being distanced from giving direct criticism to the facilitator that otherwise could feel threatening or too risky to them. It is possible to invite children to sit on the chair to become the workshop, but this is only advisable as an initial de-role activity, so the child does not take on another character and thus defeat the object of de-role.

De-role games

Many of the games and exercises used during the workshops can also be used in the de-role process. 'Anyone Who', as described in Chapter 2, is a great way of reconnecting children to their real selves. The game requires the children to speak a truth about themselves or respond by swapping places if someone else's truth applies also to them. The game can help remind children of the activities they enjoy and their feelings, thoughts and personality traits – as opposed to those of their character – and affords another opportunity for using children's real names and not their character names.

A particularly good specific de-role game is Laughing Clown. Standing in a circle, one person starts laughing to set a chain reaction around the group. The leader can change the laugh in any way they like: it might be a quiet little laugh or a great big belly laugh like a giant. Children love this activity and many will be genuinely laughing by the end; some are still smiling when they leave. I have lost count of the many children who have remarked how happy this activity has made them feel, even after exploring relatively heavy themes. And any activity that helps children feel happy can only be a good thing. An extension of this game is an activity called Just for Laughs. Everyone in the group picks out one of the following two statements from a box/hat/bag:

- I have absolutely no idea why I'm laughing.
- Laughter is the music of life.

Different statements can be used to meet different needs and age groups. The children walk around the room laughing and attempt to communicate their statement to the group through body language, eye contact, gesture and the tone and pace of their laughter. There are literally hundreds of variations of these exercises, so have fun and be creative.

Notice and adjust

Finally, part of the facilitator's role is to look out for the children in the group. If you notice that a child looks upset or distanced, sensitively feed this back to them and offer support if necessary. The games and activities, along with other exercises mentioned throughout the book, are often enough to manage the process safely. Occasionally the theme resonates with the children in unexpected ways and this requires a facilitator who can notice and adjust the activity accordingly or respond individually to the child concerned.

I will emphasize again that de-role is a non-negotiable part of the FT process; I have had to refuse requests to finish a session early without adequate de-role. If the work has been started, it should be completed with the same care and attention.

Aftercare

Aftercare support is offered universally to any of the actors or spect-actors as required: immediately after a workshop or performance session or some weeks later. Aftercare encompasses a whole range of pre-planned strategies that can support issues arising as a result of the FT, such as strategies based on:

- information about support services, charities and helplines linked to the theme

- pastoral support within the setting or commissioned from outside agencies
- follow-up focus groups, workshops or in-class/setting activities
- close liaison between parents/carers and school or setting
- advice and support from outside agencies
- in-house counselling services
- a written outline of the process and outcomes to participants and parents/carers
- noticing potential issues arising and making early adjustments.

This is an indicative rather than exhaustive list of possible aftercare activities. Aftercare plans should be mindful of the actor and spect-actor groups you may see daily, but also the audience members you may never meet again. It is ideal for audience members to at least be able to take some information away with them about sources of help and support if required. Aftercare plans should be:

- discussed as part of the setting-up of an FT project
- led by the project facilitator but agreed and supported by managers within the setting
- actively implemented at the appropriate and agreed times.

FT can be helpful in supporting children to explore a range of issues they might face. In this extract, taken from a discussion after a play, these spect-actors explain how much they enjoyed the FT experience. In particular, the children place a high value on finding potential solutions for the protagonist and themselves:

> **Y5SA:** I liked how you could, um, actually sort it out and, and you could get up and play Phoebe and stuff like that.
>
> **NH:** That's useful, that's really good. Anything else that you particularly liked about it?
>
> **Y4SA:** Eh … allowing the children to get up and have a go.

As the post-play discussions continued, the following extract shows the children left the forum feeling optimistic, despite any earlier worries:

> **NH:** … when you left the forum theatre, did you still feel worried?
>
> **Y3SA:** [immediate response] Nope.
>
> **NH:** You didn't?

Y3SA: No.

NH: ... why do you think you didn't feel worried?

Y5SA: It made me more confident ...

However, FT is unlikely to stop children from worrying altogether and there is undoubtedly some risk of the play inducing additional worries. One child who took part as a spect-actor in the Transition Project described how one of the vignettes made him wonder about whether his friends might only be pretending to be his friend:

NH: Was there anything else that you thought or felt?

Y3SA: Maybe friends ... were really tricking me to be friends and maybe just being a bit mean. And like staging me up.

FT poses some measurable risk of children feeling worried about the content of the play or leaving with unresolved concerns that weren't present before. These risks constitute another reason why time should be given after the forum if a vignette or part of the play has not been worked through, and adequate de-role provided. The risks associated with FT can be further reduced by offering support via the aftercare plan. Aftercare plans explain the planned strategies and support in place to meet any residual needs among actors, spect-actors, or audience members following an FT project. Some of these strategies used in the Transition and Empathy projects are discussed next.

Risk assessment

Most people working with children will be used to risk assessments. They are designed to identify the potential risks of a planned activity for individuals and groups of children. Risk assessments would typically provide enough information to answer these questions:

- What is the risk?
- How might harm be caused?
- Who is at risk?
- What is already in place to manage this type of risk?
- How can the risk be reduced?
- Who needs to complete the relevant action points? By when?

The level of risk is also an issue. A very low risk might be indicated, but it's impossible to remove risk altogether. There was a very high risk that children were likely to have an initial increase in worries relating to the themes of the projects discussed here. However, risk can be managed through the process of externalization and finding solutions, and further reduced by means of de-role. But despite the safety measures some children could leave with residual anxieties and these need to be managed through effective aftercare.

The awareness of adults

It is important that parents, carers and other adults responsible for the welfare of the children are aware of the possible risks of FT projects. When requesting consent for children to participate, the potential risks and benefits of taking part should be explained, whether by letter or via an information event. Adults could be invited to participate as spect-actors or watch the process as part of a broader audience and be given information about the aftercare support available.

De-brief

This takes place after the FT project, to try to ascertain what the children thought and felt during the process and afterwards. The extracts in this book offer useful clues as to the support required and for whom. In the Transition and Empathy projects, parents and carers were invited to an information event when it was over. The goal was to share outcomes and consider how these could inform future projects, and adults were offered the opportunity to ask questions and highlight any issues arising.

Signposting

It is helpful to have a list of organizations and charities that offer support and information around the theme. Depending on the theme, the age of the children and the setting, possible services might include:

- The Anti-Bullying Alliance
- Beat Bullying
- Samaritans
- Mind
- Young Minds
- ChildLine/NSPCC
- In-house counselling services
- Designated key worker, teacher or similar.

Support services

Some schools already work with outside support agencies, such as educational psychology services, behaviour support teams, autism teams and so on. Drama students will be linked to a university or college that might be able to offer support such as tutor supervision. Sharing plans with such professionals can be helpful at the risk assessment stage. Remember that while FT may bring concerns to the surface, these concerns were already there and could later manifest as problematic. This does not mean the facilitator's responsibility is negated; on the contrary, working in this way means facilitators have a duty of care to participants and this includes working in collaboration with others to offer aftercare support.

In reality, the need for ongoing aftercare is rare. Most children will be quite happy with their experience and perfectly able to separate reality from the play. Many of these children will find FT overwhelmingly favourable in terms of outcomes. However, the needs of the children will differ in each context and FT can be unpredictable in that the play will resonate with the children in different ways. Each child arrives with their own histories, and seemingly minor issues in the play could be significant for them.

Safeguarding

For a project I ran with teenagers on the theme of relationships, a play was developed with young professional actors and focused on a group of friends, one of whom presented as insecure. She had broken up with her boyfriend – who was now seeing her best friend, which was awkward – and she had become worryingly concerned about her body image. During the forum element a spect-actor stopped the action and a discussion started around the presenting challenges. Then a young man put his hand up and began to explain why he believed our protagonist could be considering self-harm. Nothing in the play suggested that self-harm was likely so it was possible that this young man was sharing something about himself. I can reassure readers that in the many hundreds of FT projects I have run with children and young people, this is a rare occurrence. However, this incident illustrates why safeguarding must be considered at all stages of FT. In this particular project we worked closely with staff in the setting who watched the play and the spect-actors' contributions. A follow-up conversation allowed our team to share our concerns with staff so they would be in a position to implement aftercare plans for this young man and follow their own safeguarding protocols.

While it is very unusual for a disclosure to surface during an FT project, this can vary depending on the population taking part. Disclosure may be explicit – a child explains that they or others are at risk of harm – or implicit, through the process of externalization, which can be more difficult to spot. So it is important to:

- familiarize yourself with the safeguarding protocols of the setting
- identify the person responsible for safeguarding in the setting

- document the process of character and narrative development. For example, if a disclosure is made, it is at least plausible that aspects of the child's experience may have been projected into a character or narrative within the play. Thus, documentation could provide evidence for any future investigation and, at the very least, offers a context to others.

Above all, if you are concerned, tell someone – preferably the person responsible for safeguarding. Even if the comment seems trivial, it's best documented and passed on, as we can never know everything about the children we work with.

It is also important to ensure the children are told that their contributions will not remain confidential, since it is impossible to stop participants from discussing work that has taken place in workshops or the performance. If a child discloses information you think may put them or others at risk of harm, the child must be told that this information will be shared with a named adult and then passed on to the person responsible for safeguarding. Even when this information has been passed on, the facilitator and others with this information still have a legal responsibility to follow-up how it has been used and to do all they reasonably can to ensure that the child and others remain protected from harm.

If you are a visitor to a setting it might be helpful to arrange a de-brief (feedback) session after the FT with a key member of staff, such as the person responsible for safeguarding, the setting manager or the head teacher. Sometimes the information shared means nothing to the FT facilitator but when put together with other information could highlight a child in need or at risk. Staff at the setting will have a perspective on the children that visitors will not have, so a feedback session is needed to bring together the different vantage points and thus help ensure the children are kept safe.

The impact of FT in the community

Aftercare support may also entail linking the FT project to broader community aims and objectives. FT is a form of social theatre so should always have a social purpose. It is likely to raise issues for discussion, address personal or systemic challenges or disempowerment, and make those in a position of power aware of the impact surrounding a theme. The social purpose of FT is especially important when working with children. The Transition Project raised issues around the school appeals system and the challenges the children faced from key adults. The challenge of transition was explored in detail from the perspective of the children in front of adults who were in a position to effect change. The hope is that while children are empowered by the opportunity to find solutions, the adults, too, review policy and practice and make amendments based on outcomes from the process. FT should aim to have outcomes beyond the project that positively affect the children who played the actors and spect-actors and their community.

The nature of community

By its very nature, FT relies on community to achieve its social purpose and this community can be far-reaching. In his ecological systems theory, psychologist Urie Bronfenbrenner offers a neat way of showing the complexities of how the child interlinks with its community. Bronfenbrenner describes how each person exists within increasingly complex micro- to macro-systems: the family and extended family, classroom and school, friendship groups and peers, policies within their school or other setting and local and national government. Enriching it all are the culture, values, beliefs and customs of their town, region and country.

FT for children begins by focusing on the concerns of the individual or a selected micro-community – the actor group. These children belong to the immediate community, the drama group, youth centre, outpatient mental health unit, pupil referral unit or some other setting, and thus provide context, sentiment, and feeling that are unique to where they live. The created play is then shared with a group of spect-actors and people from the wider community. The actor group should be easily identifiable but the spect-actor and broader audience may be varied and less obvious. If the FT project focuses on bullying, the spect-actor community would include those who have experienced bullying and at risk of being bullied. The broader audience – who may at some point become spect-actors – could be teachers, youth workers, police officers, voluntary agencies or internet safety officers, among others. Alternatively, plays could be performed to an open audience at theatre festivals or open days or as street theatre. The make-up of the spect-actor group and wider audience will depend on the content of the play, the setting and the social purpose.

All FT projects run within political and systemic climates and these determine the flexibility to run a project, the way it is run, who it is run by, with whom it is run, the themes covered and the discussions that can take place. Thus, the child's eco-system is essential as it provides opportunity and nuances that will be reflected in the play, the resolutions and the success of the project.

The social purpose of FT

FT should aim to have a lasting impact on the community in which the project is taking place. This might be explicit, such as trying to change a policy or approach to particular issues, or it might be implicit, raising awareness or using the children's views to guide decision-making. In any event, the intended impact has a social purpose.

The Transition Project addressed a range of dilemmas and challenges, the support children needed to overcome these challenges, and the role adults could play. One social purpose was to provoke teachers to consider whether changes could be made to the current transition support packages: to encourage parents to consider the impact of school applications and outcomes if their children were not to secure a place at the school of perceived prestige; and to urge local authority representatives to consider the impact of appeals systems and the stress these can cause children. The Empathy Project's main social purpose was to consider how children think, feel and act toward bullies and the bullied and the impact this has on children's well-being and school policy. FT was a way for children and adults to share how behaviour they regarded as bullying could be addressed in constructive ways. It gave outside support services a chance to offer options for building on the school's successes.

Social purposes could concern health, domestic violence, knife crime, gangs and anti-social behaviour, stranger danger, road safety, media representations of body image, homelessness, homophobia, racism and Islamophobia and other social issues relevant to the setting. Each community is different but the social purpose will guide the choice of who is to participate as spect-actors or attend the performance as general audience members.

FT may also be used as a way of exploring themes of relevance to the community. These types of themes are generated by someone within the community, such as a head teacher, who has something they want to understand about their community context. For example, a head teacher may be interested in finding out how to optimize children's learning experiences in school. Here an FT project could explore the challenges children face at school – to create the play – and the forum could offer valuable starting points for developing policy, changing approaches and working toward optimizing the learning experiences of children in school. Used in this way, the FT sets up a research community (RC), answering questions and searching out sustainable solutions to contextually relevant problems. The RC group, like the actor group, is made up of children in the community who are empowered to explore the theme in detail and, along with spect-actors, present possible ways forward to those who commissioned the work, such as the head teacher.

Social change depends on the socio-political context and organization in which the FT or performance takes place (Kershaw, 1992). So if adult observers or the spect-actors are not receptive to learning from the experience, or if the organization is too limited to implement change or too susceptible to central government pressure, then the social purpose may be more difficult to achieve.

That does not mean it *cannot* be achieved. Some readers may find themselves in a situation where they want to be an agent of change but feel restricted – a sentiment I have, on many occasions, shared. The key is to seek opportunities: these may present as 'diamonds in the rough'. Work on your links with allies, but don't sell your soul – good allies do exist and could be an organization or individual who shares your vision. You may well be attempting to do work that is on the fringes of your profession or setting. My advice is to be bold but reflective – it's at the fringes that innovative work is created. Find strength in small successes *and* failures – every experience is a learning opportunity, so even if your idea doesn't work out it's been successful if you take something from it. Your eventual FT project may not create a fanfare throughout the community in which you operate – some may even try to dismantle your hard work with criticism or cynicism. While you should take from these comments what is useful and evidenced objectively, bear in mind that not immediately securing a major social impact does not mean you have not made a significant impact at the individual level – which is equally valid. Drama may not change *the* world, but it might change *somebody's* world.

Benefits of FT in the community as part of aftercare

The benefits of the Transition Project to the community were predominantly focused on micro-systems such as friendships, family, classroom and school development. All of the children were allowed to take ownership and leadership in how they wished to share their concerns, experiences and anxieties around each sub-theme. FT allows the community to become involved with aftercare support as well as taking steps to reduce the anxieties of children who will move schools in the future.

Because FT for children is based on the collective values, beliefs and culture of the setting and wider community, ongoing support and problem-solving are more sustainable as the community has a vested interest in the outcomes and ownership of the process. And future FT projects could possibly work with issues within the community that had been hidden. In such cases, FT intervention may become circular and feel more like a lively RC or like action research, where objectives are planned, explored, tested-out in practice and documented in a circular fashion, with each cycle building on the last. This allows communities to continue to build on what is working well and intervene early where improvements are needed.

The FT project may also be developed around a special event such as a mental health awareness day or anti-bullying week or linked to an ongoing PSHE theme. This can be particularly helpful as part of aftercare because the whole school community is involved and the children have a tangible point of reference in the play. PSHE is likely to be a little trickier to manage if it is outside the school environment, and in such cases links with the wider community and other relevant agencies such as the police and youth workers may be required.

Chapter 5

Resources and materials for a forum theatre project

Teaching is a very demanding profession, often with lots of competing priorities. Myself, and many teachers I know, are always open to new and exciting ideas, but implementing new ideas is made easier when there are resources available, such as lesson plans, to help. So for me, practical resources are really important.

(Trainee primary teacher)

Introduction

This book has set out to empower professionals, such as teachers, to utilize FT in their own setting. It recognizes that practitioners are often so busy with their everyday workload that it can feel difficult to take on new ways of working. This chapter attempts to facilitate the implementation of FT by offering practical advice and resources. The resources cover the different aspects of FT and are presented in two sections: 'Timeline of events' and 'Working with FT'.

Timeline of events: Starting the process

Timelines are likely to vary depending on your needs and setting. An FT project can be run in as little as one day, as was the Empathy Project, while others require weeks, months or even years. The Transition Project was run over five weeks and is the model outlined here. It allowed the children time to explore the theme in some depth and learn the techniques required to perform in FT more fully. Each workshop and performance lasted two hours; a good amount of time for a full-scale FT project and commendable in light of the competing priorities of the curriculum (although you can adjust these timings to suit your own setting, of course). A five-week project timeline is presented in Table 5.1.

Table 5.1 Timeline of events based on a five-week project

	Activity	Resources	Objectives
Preliminary	• Commission project • Identify theme • Identify actor group • Identify timescales, space and other logistics • Risk assessment • Parent/child consent • Design aftercare plan	• *Benefits of FT* sheet • Risk assessment sheet • Parent consent form • The timetable within your setting • Room booking form – if required	• To establish a commitment from the Senior Management Team and parents to support an FT project • To recruit a group of children who identify with the theme • To begin to create a safe project and identify risks
Weeks 1–4	• Workshops with de-role	• A space • Activities described in this book • Your own drama-based activities as required	• To develop characters and narrative • To devise a play around the theme • To rehearse the play and FT techniques
Week 5	• Final workshop • Performance with de-role • Implement aftercare including feedback to parents/carers	• A space • Activities identified in this book • Your own drama-based activities as required • Aftercare materials including protected time to follow-up issues arising	• To complete final rehearsals • To perform the play to spect-actors with the aim of finding solutions to the undesirable ending of the play • To continue to support issues arising for actors, spect-actors and audience members

Risk assessment

Potential risks, and the actions required to reduce those risks, need to be identified as far as possible. The assessments used in the Empathy and Transition projects are outlined in Table 5.2. You can create and make copies of a blank form with the same column headings (Identified risk, Nature of risk etc.) to use when planning your own FT project.

Table 5.2 Sample risk assessment

Identified risk	Nature of risk	Action taken to reduce risk	Remaining risk
Consent	Parents and children will need to understand the nature of FT and proposed outcomes in order to make an informed decision.	Information sheet sent to parents and children. Opportunity offered to contact facilitator to discuss any concerns.	Low risk
Right to withdraw	Parents and children have the right to withdraw from the project at any time without giving a reason. After a certain time withdrawal may not be possible. (This is only relevant where you are conducting research and will be processing data in relation to your project. If this is the case be sure to reflect this in the consent form.)	Information sheet and ongoing opportunities to withdraw from the project.	Low risk

Identified risk	Nature of risk	Action taken to reduce risk	Remaining risk
Physical harm	A fall during games and activities that could result in injury. Possibility of disclosure.	Ensuring activity is explained clearly and limitations set to ensure activity is as safe as possible – such as in games where a blindfold is used, children are told not to run and to listen carefully. To set ground rules that outline responsibility for each other. Ensure space is clear of any tripping hazards. Follow agreed safeguarding policy and procedure.	Low risk
Psychological harm	Children may experience anxiety thinking about difficulties related to the theme. Spect-actors and audience may feel uncomfortable with challenges presented. Some stress related to the devising and performance of the play. Possibility of disclosure.	Managed through de-role and aftercare support. Good liaison with setting staff. Utilizing the full FT process, including allowing children who have not worked through their vignette to complete this task at a pre-agreed future date.	Low risk

Identified risk	Nature of risk	Action taken to reduce risk	Remaining risk
		Using theatre games and activities to reduce stress at the devising and performance stage, including the huddle. Following safeguarding policy and procedure.	
Confidentiality	It is not possible to ensure complete confidentiality.	Children in the actor group and their parents are told that confidentiality cannot be guaranteed. Actors are steered away from simply replicating real issues toward using sentiment and emotion from those experiences.	Medium risk

Consent and information sheet for parents

Parent/carer consent and information sheets can be tricky to compile. Every setting is different and some parents/carers may be illiterate. Thus it is helpful to hold, in addition, a short information event that covers the same points as a traditional consent and information sheet. The template version of an information sheet and consent form, shown next, are based on those used in the Transition and Empathy projects. The blank spaces are for you to fill in based on your setting and project design.

Information sheet

1. **Title of FT project:**
2. **Invitation to participate**
   Your child has been invited to take part in the above project. It is important that you understand the purpose of the project and what is involved before you decide whether to give consent for your child's participation. Please read the information carefully. Feel free to discuss this information with the project leader or ask questions at any time. Thank you for your time and consideration.
3. **The background and purpose of the project**
   This will cover who the project leader is and the theme of the FT.

4. **What is forum theatre (FT)?**
   FT has been extensively used in a wide range of settings. The aim is to work in workshops with a small group of people who have a particular theme in common concerning, for example, relationships or a shared situation. In the workshops the group explore their chosen theme and the challenges that might exist as part of it. In the project your child has been invited to participate in, we will look at the theme of

   _____.

   The workshops will equip the group with certain theatre techniques. The aim is to develop a play that ends with the main character facing a challenge related to the agreed theme of the project. The play is then shown to an audience who are invited to suggest solutions to help the main character overcome their challenge. Everyone involved in the FT will have the opportunity to:

   - explore their thoughts and feelings about the theme
   - work together to find real solutions to the challenge
   - develop social, emotional and cognitive skills
   - learn from others.

5. **Why has my child been chosen?**
   This explains how participants in the actor group have been identified as having the particular theme in common.

6. **Does my child have to take part?**
   No. Taking part is entirely voluntary and all participants have the right to withdraw at any time. If you do decide your child can participate, you will need to sign the consent form enclosed with this sheet. Your decision will not affect aspects of your child's schooling in any other respect, and you do not have to give a reason for your decision. Your child will also be asked to give consent and their rights to withdraw at any time will be explained.

7. **What will my child experience if they take part in the FT?**
   This will depend on the group your child participates in. If your child is in the actor group, they will be asked to participate in ___ (*number*) workshops and perform their work to an audience. The workshops will explore the theme of _____ and equip children with the skills they need to perform. The workshops will take place at _____ for __ hours. If your child participates as a member of the audience, they will be actively involved during the performance element of the project. The performance will take place on _____ at _____.
   Exact times will be confirmed nearer the performance day.

8. **What are the possible disadvantages and risks for my child taking part?**
   This will cover the risks as identified in the risk assessment.

   • Possible initial feelings of anxiety or stress when considering the challenges relevant to the theme, as the theme intentionally focuses on an issue known to be of concern to the children.
   •
   •
   •

9. **What are the likely benefits of taking part?** *This will cover the benefits already identified and others that are specific to the setting/project.*

   • An enjoyable and fun experience
   • An opportunity to develop social, emotional and cognitive skills

- A child-centred learning experience
- An opportunity to develop transferable skills such as team work and confidence
- An opportunity to understand certain challenges that children face related to the theme of (*specify theme* _____)
-
-
-

10. **What happens if the project stops earlier than expected?**
In the event of the project dates changing, the timeline being adjusted or the project being cancelled, an explanation will be given to all participants, parents/carers and staff.

11. **What if something goes wrong?**
If you are concerned or would like to make a complaint about how the project is being handled, the participant or their legal guardian can contact the project leader directly:

Name:
Address:
Email address:
Contact telephone number:

12. **Will my child's taking part in this project be kept confidential?**
Any personal details recorded about you or your child will be kept in accordance with the Data Protection Act 1998. However, the nature of the project means that it is not possible to guarantee confidentiality regarding issues or experiences arising as a result of participation.

13. **How will I find out the outcome of the project?** *This will cover what feedback is planned for parents/carers after the project. This might include a written, verbal or display board summary.*

Consent form
Title of project:

Name of project leader:

1. I confirm that I have read and understood the information sheet attached for the above project and have had the opportunity to ask questions. I agree that my child can participate in the project as described.
2. I understand that my child's participation is voluntary and that my child is free to withdraw at any time without giving a reason.

All children who are asked to take part in the workshops will also be asked by the facilitator to give their consent.

Name of child: _____   **Year Group:** _____

Signature of parent/legal guardian:

_____

Print name of parent/legal guardian:

_____

If you have any questions or would like further information on any aspect of this project please contact:

Name:
Address:
Email address:
Contact telephone number:

Working with FT: Storyboard model template and lesson plan

FT prefers the development of a model that sets out a linear sequence of events, rather than a traditional script. The model can be a bullet-point list of sequenced events or a drawn storyboard like the one shown in Chapter 1 (Figure 1.3). This approach has proved to be helpful, since the activity of drawing key sequences allows for consolidation and cognitive rehearsal of how the play will run. You can create a blank template using the layout in Figure 1.3. The larger boxes are intended for the children to draw the scene in, while the small boxes underneath are for either the adult or children to create a caption that summarizes what happens in the scene. The caption may include key words or phrases used by the character(s).

Lesson plan using explorative FT

FT is not a lesson but an experience in which learning can take place. It is not intended to have prescriptive outcomes like a national curriculum. This is because the aim is to explore the theme under investigation rather than the adult teaching, telling or disseminating knowledge. However, even in flexible curriculum subjects such as PSHE or in drama clubs or youth centres, adults are still likely to need some documentation to indicate their objectives, purpose and potential outcomes, be it for Ofsted, commissioners or external funders. In this sense, a lesson plan is not solely a document for school or other educational settings, but also more broadly usable.

When using FT, lesson plans need to stipulate the following:

- **Date/time/location**: Where and when?
- **Theme and relevance**: What makes your group homogeneous and the theme pertinent?
- **Resources**: What do you need?
- **Activities**: What will you and the group do? And in what order?
- **Intended outcomes**: What do you hope will be the outcome?
- **Success criteria**: How will you know if the outcomes have been achieved?
- **Reflective objectives**: What have we learnt through the FT exploration?

Table. 5.3 shows a completed sample lesson plan for a typical workshop. Each workshop and the performance will have slightly different learning outcomes, so it's likely you will have a different lesson plan for each part of the project. You can create your own blank form using these headings when planning your own FT project.

Table 5.3 Sample lesson plan

Date: --/--/-- Time: 13:00–15:00 Location: School Hall

Theme and relevance: The theme is transition. Y6 pupils are taking part in the actor group as transition to secondary school is imminent. Preliminary discussions have highlighted other relevant sub-themes including personal experiences of divorce, parents separating, moving home, moving country and seeing siblings move to secondary school.

Resources	Activities
• A space big enough for drama-based activities • Agreed ground rules for the group • Adult facilitator and Y6 group • Drama-based activities based on exploration, experience and other identified resources • Chairs • Props box containing random items of costume and objects	• A selection of warm-up activities – partly to be decided by the group • Character and narrative activities. This week introduce tableau, Yeti Language, free writing and story circle • Various de-role activities
Intended outcomes	**Success criteria**
• To maintain a safe space • To develop an awareness of character development • To help children understand narrative and how it might be used	• Evaluation circle feedback and successful de-role • Develop at least one character to whom the children can attribute motivation, thoughts and feelings • Create a simple narrative specifically through the use of Yeti Language and a storytelling circle

Reflective objectives: In this workshop all intended outcomes were reached. In addition the children were able to explore the theme through the eyes of the characters they played. The children demonstrated the ability to critically explore the theme by posing questions and taking on different roles.

Chapter 6

The road less travelled: The unanswered questions and research potential of FT

Introduction

This book has shown how FT can be an empowering experience that can support the development of social, emotional, cognitive and creative skills among children. Using examples from past FT projects to illustrate psychological frameworks in action, I have detailed how FT can be run in a way that optimizes outcomes for all those involved. However, some questions remain unanswered and this chapter seeks to highlight these gaps in our knowledge.

FT remains popular because it affords empowering opportunities for individual and collective exploration of relevant issues and can point the way to desirable change in relation to a given theme. Students and professionals alike continue to be interested in the nature and potential of FT as a research method and way of working. This final chapter offers some additional practical activities and poses potential research questions for student or practitioner researchers to consider when using FT.

Exploring the individual and group experience of FT

FT is bound to be experienced differently by each child. Some of these differences will be self-evident, for instance whether they experience the FT as an actor or spect-actor. Boal believed that an FT experience will hold a different meaning for each person who observes or interacts with the play. As we have seen, the children externalize their own anxieties and concerns through role play, discussion and finding solutions. But these personal thoughts become owned by the group as they resonate with, and are influenced by, the other children. This raises an interesting question: how does a child experience FT as an individual and does this differ from the experience as part of a group?

During the Transition Project there was evidence that children shared concerns about separating from friends and being bullied, yet the follow-up discussions showed very different stories and experiences being brought to the FT. The children were able to recognize their individual experiences – their own stories – while at the same time assuming a common ground with their peers over the general sub-themes of bullying or separating from friends, thus indicating that FT is both an individual and a group experience. As the play resonates on a group level, the individual's attitudes, perceptions, actions and suggestions will be refined and self-edited to better fit with the group direction. Although a child may wish to address a particular nuance within the play, if the group direction is different they may refrain from focusing on it, whether this issue is important to them or not. This is the phenomenon of group conformity.

Psychologist Soloman Asch carried out a series of infamous experiments on this phenomenon that demonstrated how, when people are part of a group, the majority generally rules. In these simple experiments Asch presented a group with four vertical lines of different heights. However, the group was made up of research assistants and only one subject. Asch asked which line was the shortest and although the answer was obvious, the research assistants all gave the same incorrect response. The single real participant gave the same incorrect response, despite knowing the response was wrong. This experiment has been repeated many times over, generally with the same result: the real participant conforms to the group norm by knowingly giving an incorrect response. So how does group conformity impact on the direction of the FT and the decisions taken along the way?

The questions surrounding group experiences of FT become more intriguing when the work of psychologist Wilfred Bion is taken into account. Bion argued that all groups gather to create change through action of some kind (Bion, 1961). Bion also claimed that dynamics within the group can alter how participants experience phenomena, in this case FT. Bion outlined significant group dynamics such as:

- **Fight-or-flight groups:** Some children intend to fight the challenges of transition, while others may try to escape by not engaging directly with the challenges presented. This may result in some children being enthused and keen to attempt change while others appear to be indifferent.
- **Dependence groups:** The group may look to the facilitator to maintain the FT or act as a driver for change. But if they look to the facilitator to teach them what they need to know it defeats the purpose of FT.
- **Pairing groups or splinter groups:** Children form alliances within the group, making the group difficult to manage. This pattern is more

likely to occur among community-based groups such as youth centres, where alliances in the community may already exist – for example, in the form of allegiance to the local postcode that is common in gang cultures across parts of Britain. A more subtle but common example is that of alliances based on gender – boys and girls not wanting to work together.

Each dynamic within the group could lead to different challenges and opportunities. Pairing groups may be more inclined to offer counter-oppressive solutions based on in-group/out-group values and beliefs, as we saw in the Bullying Project. Fight-or-flight groups may create split decisions, although group consensus can usually be established by taking a vote, but the dominant group could prevent this from happening or respond apathetically. The dependency group may seek a director's cut of how everything ought to be by the end of the play. However, ideally we want all FT groups to take ownership of the play and find their own solutions to increase sustainability in the community; a group that is over-dependent on outside influences is unlikely to achieve this.

The following research questions arise in relation to how the FT is experienced:

- How far does group conformity impact on the individual's experience of FT?
- How can we best identify patterns in group dynamics and respond to the three group experiences outlined by Bion?
- Are group experiences different in each FT project or does there tend to be a pattern of group behaviour?
- How might the group process impact on the individual's experience of FT and subsequent outcomes?
- How does the group dynamic impact on how the FT is facilitated? What can the facilitator do to optimize the experience for the group and for each individual?

The role of the facilitator

Exactly what is happening, in emotional and psycho-analytic terms, in the interaction between the facilitator and the actors/spect-actors is not particularly well understood. The facilitator could be regarded as the group leader, but technically this does not accurately sum up the facilitator's role. In the actor group the facilitator sets up activities, but the children quickly take the lead in how the activities inform their creations of both the story and characters. In the spect-actor group, the facilitator introduces the play, poses questions and supports the actor group in their improvisations. Again, the children take the lead in finding solutions and the facilitator's role is to mediate. We can see the interaction between the children and the facilitator as a metaphorical dance, where both the children and the facilitator can lead and be led and where they can also have individual solos and collective ensembles.

What is more intriguing about the facilitator–group dynamic is the subtleties of the interaction and how these are acted-on in the moment. For example, during the Transition Project children offered what seemed quite straightforward solutions, but which proved, on further exploration, to be quite complex. One idea shared by a child to challenge bullying, as we saw in an earlier chapter, was to step aside when the bully passed along the corridor. Hidden nuances within this solution such as the power of silence, the passive disarming of the bully, the confusion of the bully's thoughts and the feelings of the protagonist were some of the complexities that arose. Psychologists refer to the reduction of complex ideas into a smaller single idea as condensation. How does the facilitator manage condensation in the moment? The Transition Project used a number of questions and discussions to unpack some of these ideas, but how much nuance is missed when such complex ideas are condensed? A related question that can arise for the facilitator when dealing with condensed issues is that of whose idea to take forward. The final choice to work with one idea potentially excludes several others, so when there are dominant group members there is also the potential for quieter voices to go unheard and for the facilitator to go with the more prominent theme. The facilitator must therefore not only remain alert to the condensed issues themselves but also attend to the process of unravelling them with care, to ensure the optimum outcome for the group overall.

The children arrive at an FT workshop or performance session with their own histories that shape not only the characters and the play, but also the child–facilitator relationship. The child may, through the process of transference, attribute their attitudes, feelings and thoughts about the adult figures in their own histories onto the facilitator; and the facilitator may, in turn, feel this and reciprocate by actions or feelings toward the child – a phenomenon known as counter-transference. This process is best understood through a practical example:

> A child arrives at an FT performance day at a youth centre run by a male facilitator. She carries negative feelings from her relationship with her father and projects these emotions onto

other males she perceives to have similar characteristics – such as age or personality traits. The facilitator recognizes the negative feeling from this girl, but is unlikely to be able to identify her reasons. The girl may be hostile, angry, avoidant or dismissive, although she is unaware of her projective feelings, which arise unconsciously and unintentionally. The facilitator might behave in such a way that he reinforces the child's negative feelings, perhaps such as over- or under-compensating in his interactions with her – equally unconsciously but possibly driven by feeling the child's negative attitude towards him.

It is not difficult to see how this situation could escalate and so create a completely undesirable experience of FT for both the child and the facilitator. Not all negative feeling is due to transference and counter-transference though, so it is important to understand ourselves too (Bion, 1961). Sometimes people simply do not get along as there is a personality clash. These concepts provide an interesting area for exploration around the role of the facilitator in FT and the management of micro-interactions. They also evoke certain research questions such as:

- How can the interaction between facilitator and actors/spect-actors be optimized?
- What role do transference and counter-transference play in FT interactions? How can facilitators prevent or overcome the potential disadvantages in the interactions?
- How can nuance be managed by the facilitator and Auxiliary Joker(s) in the moment, when complex ideas are reduced to a single idea or action?

Learning through experience in FT

FT is a learning tool; it can raise awareness of issues, lead to new insights and solutions and help adults better understand children's perceptions and therefore implement appropriate policies and practices. However, it is unclear how much of the learning that takes place in the FT is generalized by the children and adults who take part. The Transition Project indicated that children were reminded of previous strategies and gained new insights that made them feel more confident in overcoming transition-related challenges in their own lives, but the project did not follow up on whether they went on to apply what they had learned in the FT to real-life situations.

However, we know that FT does at least have the potential to support children in generalizing their learning. Educationalist David Kolb proposed a theory of experiential learning, or learning-through-doing, that claimed children's learning was optimized when a series of conditions were fulfilled. Taking the conditions Kolb identified one by one, I will highlight in the following summary (in italics) how FT fulfils these criteria for optimum learning:

- they are given concrete learning opportunities – *through a relevant play the issues are highly tangible*
- they can participate fully – *the play activities, discussion and observation used in FT enable active involvement*
- they have the opportunity to think about how the experience made them feel and think – *by means of aftercare and de-role support*
- they are encouraged to link new ideas from personal experience and generate potential solutions to their own problems – *the Transition Project follow-up discussions showed evidence of how this works in FT. Children have opportunities to test the new ideas generated by the FT to solve new challenges.*

The outcomes of the Transition Project show that children do expand their problem-solving repertoires as a result of FT. But does the potential of FT translate to these new problem-solving skills being used in the future when the children face their own real-life transitions?

For children to generalize from their experience, it is helpful to engage the wider community and make links to previous experiences or structures, such as linking FT to PSHE as part of aftercare plans. Linking experiences is an idea John Dewey (1938) called 'connectedness', whereby interest is sustained from the original FT, or experience, through ongoing relevant experiences and optimized when participants take ownership of the activity. Working with children as actors is one way ownership can be achieved, but ideally attempts to increase ownership will be more wide-reaching such as developing FT as an RC and linking this to the wider community. Research has shown that simply recommissioning arts experiences is unhelpful unless the community ethos maintains the experience in-between each project (Wilkin *et al.*, 2005). It is important to consider how connectedness, or generalization, can be optimized and made more likely to occur beyond FT. This may be achieved by linking your project to a pertinent issue within your setting, wider community or curriculum.

The importance of connectedness in FT does not end with achieving learning outcomes but could also help some children feel more hopeful. Behavioural psychologist Curt Richter is credited with being one of the first to observe the effects of hopelessness and hopefulness in the laboratory

(Schulkin, 2005). Researchers have found that engagement with empowering activities can lead one to learn to be hopeful (Zimmerman, 1990). Humans can learn through experience that situations are escapable and thus remain motivated in times of adversity. This is in contrast to theories of learned helplessness which find their origins in the work of behavioural psychologist Martin Seligman. One infamous study found that while escaping adverse experiences appears to be an innate response, when such experiences were presented as unavoidable – that is, the adversity would occur whether an attempt to escape were initiated or not – organisms could learn to become helpless (Seligman and Maier, 1967). Persistent failure and adversity in the classroom or community are thus likely to lead to disengagement or, in other words, a feeling of helplessness. So it is plausible that providing opportunities for children to learn to be hopeful and generalize this learning to real life – as I have found FT to encourage – can be invaluable. Evidence presented in this book would certainly support this idea, but how might teachers expand on hopefulness further? In a project based on the theme of transition it may be helpful to collaborate with pastoral staff within secondary schools perhaps, such as by developing an FT play with a group of Year Sevens for presentation to a Y6–7 audience or vice versa. But further research is needed to understand to what extent hopefulness is acquired through FT and how it can be maintained over time.

Broader research questions that can be asked about how children learn through the FT experience include:

- How are learning experiences from FT generalized to new situations?
- Do children apply solutions gathered from FT to issues in real life? If so, do they attribute these solutions to FT or to other learning experiences?
- What follow-up work can optimize generalization and connectedness?
- Who is best placed to optimize connectedness when delivering an FT project?

Development of self and the importance of role

It is impossible to imagine a human being who does not engage in taking certain roles: the parent, the worker, the carer, the child and/or the friend are among the roles most human beings assume daily, and they are able to move between different roles quickly, effortlessly and without much thought. Psychiatrist Jacob Moreno is notable for his pioneering technique known as psychodrama and his work on role theory. Moreno and Fox (1987) claim that playing different roles is a way of presenting versions of one's self. This raises the question of the impact of role-taking – a significant activity in FT – on the self, beyond a project.

To explore this question in relation to FT we must consider the nature of self and how selfhood develops from childhood. Baldwin (2001) proposes a number of developmental stages of self:

- **Projective self:** The child understands differences between people in the way they respond and their actions.
- **Subjective self:** The child becomes aware of their own body and imitates the behaviour of others. Imitation becomes more complex as cognitive ability and emotional awareness develop.
- **Reciprocal social self:** The child understands that there are differences in their experiences of the world. They develop a sense of 'me' and 'I'. Harter (1999) categorizes the I-self as subjective – about self-awareness, action and coherence – and the Me-self as objective – about the social, spiritual and material and what others can observe in me.

Parallels can be drawn between a child's development of self and an FT approach that allows children to observe, discover and rediscover versions of their self and others through role play. Accordingly, that FT could support the development of self-esteem has often been claimed. But development of a sense of self is only one part of self-esteem. Butler (2001) suggests that the sum of self-esteem is the margin between a self-rating of one's actual self (how the child sees themselves now) and one's ideal self (how the child would like to be). The smaller the gap between the child's perception of their current self and their desirable self, the higher their self-esteem.

During the Empathy Project the children's self-esteem was measured using Butler's self-esteem assessment (Butler, 2001). In this assessment children are presented with a number of statements and a scale to indicate how true or untrue each statement is to them. The children are asked to make two marks on the paper: one to indicate how true the statement is to them now (actual self) and the other to indicate where they would like to be (ideal self). Our cohort was too small to report the statistical scores but the indicative findings were rather remarkable: children with lower self-esteem generally had increased scores after the FT. An even more promising finding was that these children maintained their improvement over time. Interestingly, those with higher self-esteem at the outset either made unremarkable improvement or remained the same following the FT. Some years before the Empathy Project, I ran an FT project along with a group of touring actors on the theme of relationships. We took the FT to a further education college, where we asked the young people – who made up the spect-actor group – to complete a standardized measurement of emotional self-awareness. Those who scored below average on the scale, and who also had low academic attainment levels at the time of the project, showed notable improvements following FT. Those who scored above average on the scale made some, generally slight, progress. Follow-up scores were not taken at the college, so I cannot say whether the improvement was maintained. These findings require further exploration, but they do indicate the potential of FT's efficacy in improving self-esteem and emotional self-awareness, particularly for those whose self-esteem scores are below average before the FT. It would be interesting to explore any differences between actor and spect-actor groups and determine whether either group benefits more than the other. The use of a control group in such an investigation would add value to any findings.

Moreno's contribution to role training is under-explored in FT, although I would anticipate, given Moreno's role theory and Kelly's PCP, that rehearsal with different roles could help children understand how previous experiences impact on their responses to new situations. This could be quite transformative. Research questions relating to role can be asked, such as:

- How great is FT's efficacy at improving self-esteem and emotional self-awareness among participants?
- Is there a difference in role-taking as a spect-actor or as an actor and the resulting impact on self-esteem, emotional self-awareness and other aspects of self-development?
- How do the theatrical and psychological meanings of role interrelate and how might one inform the other during an FT project?

The use of archetypes in FT: Developing a voice and physicality for characters

Carl Jung proposed that human beings share a collective unconscious within which thousands of symbolic characters – or outlines of behaviour – exist; he called these archetypes (Jung, 1959). Archetypes are given shape and meaning when we use our imagination, and have been developed in the theatre most often through mask work. Common archetypes, or masks, include the fool, the mother and the hero – all of them instantly recognizable to the audience and each having easily identifiable physicality and characteristics (Wilsher, 2007).

Mask work can be really helpful in enabling children to experiment with role-taking. A simple mask-based game involves inviting each participant to pick the name of a child-friendly character from a hat, such as a clown – similar to the fool – monkey, penguin, astronaut, kangaroo, fairy, hero (usually used as a traditional mask too) magician or king/queen.

Each child is encouraged to think about their mask and start developing the character's physicality – their posture, mannerisms and movements – and voice. Other children in the group are encouraged to copy the mask or develop their own version. Discussions are held around what causes the character to walk or communicate in a particular way and how we change our body and voice to assume new characters. Archetype or mask work can explore how different personas might manage a challenge or view a scenario. The use of archetypes may even create an extra layer of distance and contribute to a holistic, empathetic and creative approach to overcoming challenges; but what value does this add to the FT process? This question remains unanswered, although some dramatherapists have explored Jungian links to drama-based approaches more generally.

Characters can also be developed from different perspectives without the use of archetypes. One way is by using the Emotions Exchange game. This is used in workshops to allow children to remain in their original character while approaching a scene with a different range of emotions. This can help the children to maintain the connection with their character while viewing the same material through different lenses. The Emotions Exchange game goes like this:

- Already in character, the children begin to walk around the room.
- An emotion is called out by the facilitator and the children, in character, take on the physicality and voice of that emotion – be it sad, happy, excited or scared.
- Once the children are used to swapping emotions, a scene is chosen to work on. The relevant actors take up their starting tableau.
- The scene is run and the children are encouraged to switch between emotions during their scene. Or they might play out the entire scene while expressing one emotion and then re-run the scene with a different emotion. Alternatively, the children start with one emotion, but switch to a new emotion when the facilitator claps their hands.

This can be a useful way to develop a voice and physicality for characters without using archetypes. In addition, the game can help develop awareness of physicality, voice, imagination and general performance skills. The switch of emotions will probably affect how the scene is played out or resolved. This can be quite freeing as the children have to consider the character through different emotional lenses, thus helping to explore elements that were hidden.

But archetypes should not be hastily discarded, as they provide universal representations of human behaviour. These representations are important and may support children's views of what it is to be social, allowing them to get closer to considering what it is to be the Other (as they might in role reversal). Archetypes could extend the child's ability to develop social and emotional skills within FT, but as FT is not therapy the purpose of experimenting with roles or archetypes is not to repair or heal the child's character or their sense of self. Using archetypes to explore fictional characters and develop the child's skills in performance or to give spect-actors a framework to try out new ideas could be legitimate, but research questions relating to the use of archetypes arise:

- How does switching between archetypes impact on the development or resolution of an FT play? Is it any more or less effective than using different emotions?
- How do the archetypes used in workshops allow for greater exploration of character and develop performance skills?
- How does the use of archetypes during the performance impact on the children's exploration and identification of relevant solutions?
- When does the use of archetypes have a stronger impact – in workshops or during the play?

Final reflections

This book set an ambitious and innovative challenge to draw together the fields of psychology, education and theatre in an attempt to understand the processes inherent in the FT approach. Along the way I have presented many more questions than answers. But this is the exciting nature of FT. I hope that by outlining the theory, underpinning psychology and customary practices of FT, and by taking readers through two projects step-by-step, I have encouraged you to adopt FT in your own setting.

Despite some of the challenges inherent in implementing FT, it remains an invaluable approach to working with children. FT affords children and adults the opportunity to explore complex social situations *together* and to better understand how these complexities relate to the individual and the community. It provides a basis on which the challenges associated with a situation can be overcome and allows *all* children to communicate, explore and meaning-make through play – an ever-growing novelty in today's climate of assessment, elitist academia and unreasonable expectation. In essence we are talking about allowing children to be children through serious play. And this, as has been shown, is of major importance for all adults who genuinely care that children are empowered in the development of policy, practice and life-decisions that impact on them directly.

References

Action for Children (2010) *Deprivation and Risk: The case for early intervention.* London: Action for Children. Online. www.actionforchildren.org.uk/media/139941/deprivation_and_risk_the_case_for_early_intervention.pdf (accessed 10 October 2014).

Allport, G.W. (1979) *The Nature of Prejudice.* Jackson, TN: Perseus.

Babbage, F. (2004) *Augusto Boal.* London: Routledge.

Baldwin, J.M. (2001) *Social and Ethical Interpretations in Mental Development: A study in social psychology.* New York: Adamant Media Corporation.

Bandura, A., Ross, D., and Ross, S.A. (1963) 'Imitation of film-mediated aggressive models'. *Journal of Abnormal and Social Psychology*, 66 (1), 3–11.

Beisser, A.R. (1970) 'The paradoxical theory of change'. In Fagan, J. and Shepherd, I. (eds), *Gestalt Therapy Now: Theory, techniques, applications.* Gouldsboro, ME: Gestalt Journal Press.

Bion, W.R. (1961) *Experiences in Groups and Other Papers.* London: Tavistock.

Boal, A. (1979) *Theatre of the Oppressed.* London: Pluto Press.

— (1995) *The Rainbow of Desire: The Boal method of theatre and therapy.* London: Routledge.

— (2002) *Games for Actors and Non-Actors.* London: Routledge.

Butler, R. (2001) *The Self Image Profiles for Children* [SIP-C]. London: The Psychological Corporation.

Clark, A. (1997) *Being There: Putting brain, body and world together again.* Cambridge, MA: MIT Press.

Clegg, J., and Hartshorne, M. (2004) 'Speech and language therapy in hyperactivity: A United Kingdom perspective in complex cases'. *Seminars in Speech and Language*, 25 (3), 263–70. Online. www.thieme-connect.com/products/ejournals/abstract/10.1055/s-2004-833674 (accessed 10 October 2014).

Cooper, N., and Dumpleton, S. (2013) *Walking the Breadline: The scandal of food poverty in 21st century Britain.* London: Church Action on Poverty/Oxfam. Online. www.church-poverty.org.uk/walkingthebreadline/info/report/walkingthebreadlinefile (accessed 10 October 2014).

De Bono, E. (1970) *Lateral Thinking: A textbook of creativity.* London: Ward Lock Educational.

— (1986) *Six Thinking Hats.* London: Viking.

Delaney, M. (2010) *What Can I Do About the Kid Who...? A teachers' quick guide to dealing with disruptive pupils (and their parents).* Duffield: Worth Publishing.

Department for Children, Schools and Families (2008) *Targeted Mental Health in Schools Project: Using the evidence to inform your approach. A practical guide for headteachers and commissioners.* Nottingham: DCSF. http://www.chimat.org.uk/resource/item.aspx?RID=61178

— (2009) *Deprivation and Education: The evidence on pupils in England, Foundation Stage to Key Stage 4.* London: DCSF. Online. www.gov.uk/government/publications/deprivation-and-education-the-evidence-on-pupils-in-england-foundation-stage-to-key-stage-4

Department for Education (2013a) *The National Curriculum in England: Key Stages 1 and 2 framework document*. London: DfE. Online. www.gov.uk/government/publications/national-curriculum-in-england-framework-for-key-stages-1-to-4

— (2013b) *The National Curriculum in England: Key Stages 3 and 4 framework document*. London: DfE. www.gov.uk/government/uploads/system/uploads/attachment_data/file/330327/SECONDARY_national_curriculum_FINAL_140714.pdf

Department of Health (2011) *No Health without Mental Health*: *A cross-government mental health outcomes strategy for people of all ages*. London: DoH. www.gov.uk/government/uploads/system/uploads/attachment_data/file/213761/dh_124058.pdf

De Shazer, S., and Dolan, Y. (2007) *More Than Miracles: The state of the art of solution-focused brief therapy*. Binghamton, NY: Haworth Press.

Dewey, J. (1938) *Experience and Education*. New York: Macmillan.

Dunlosky, J., and Metcalfe, J. (2009) *Metacognition: A textbook for cognitive, educational, life span and applied psychology*. Thousand Oaks, CA: Sage.

Ecclestone, K., and Hayes, D. (2009) *The Dangerous Rise of Therapeutic Education*. London: Routledge.

Fagan, J. and Shepherd, I.L. (2006) *Gestalt Therapy Now: Theory, techniques, applications*. Gouldsboro, ME: The Gestalt Journal Press.

Fernald, A., Marchman, V.A. and Weisleder, A. (2013) 'SES differences in language processing skills and vocabulary are evident at 18 months'. *Developmental Science*, 16, 234–48. Online. http://onlinelibrary.wiley.com/doi/10.1111/desc.12019/full (accessed 10 October 2014).

Freire, P. (1993) *Pedagogy of the Oppressed*. New York: Continuum.

Hammond, N. (2013) 'Introducing forum theatre to elicit and advocate children's views'. *Educational Psychology in Practice*, 29, 1–18. Online. www.tandfonline.com/doi/abs/10.1080/02667363.2012.733309#.VDfiVhaVB8M (accessed 10 October 2014).

Harter, S. (1999) *The Construction of the Self: A developmental perspective*. New York: Guilford Press.

Jung, C.G. (1959) *The Archetypes and the Collective Unconscious*. Princeton: Princeton University Press. Vol. 9, Part 1 of *The Collected Works of C.G. Jung*, 20 vols, 1957–79.

Kelly, G. (1963) *A Theory of Personality: The psychology of personal constructs*. New York: W.W. Norton.

Kershaw, B. (1992) *The Politics of Performance: Radical theatre as cultural intervention*. London: Routledge.

Kolb, D.A. (1984) *Experiential Learning: Experience as the source of learning and development*. Englewood Cliffs, NJ: Prentice-Hall.

Langley, D. (2006) *An Introduction to Dramatherapy*. London: Sage.

Locke, A., Ginsborg, J. and Peers, I. (2002) 'Development and disadvantage: Implications for the early years and beyond'. *International Journal of Language and Communication Disorders*, 37 (1), 3–15. Online. http://informahealthcare.com/doi/abs/10.1080/13682820110089911 (accessed 10 October 2014).

McFarlane, P. (2005) *Dramatherapy: Developing emotional stability*. London: David Fulton.

Milton, J., Polmear, C., and Fabricius, J. (2004) *A Short Introduction to Psychoanalysis.* London: Sage.

Moreno, J.L., and Fox, J. (1987) *The Essential Moreno: Writings on psychodrama, group method, and spontaneity.* New York: Springer.

Perkins, S.C., Finegood, E.D., and Swain, J.E. (2013) 'Poverty and language development: Roles of parenting and stress'. *Innovations in Clinical Neuroscience,* 10, 10–19. Online. www.ncbi.nlm.nih.gov/pmc/articles/PMC3659033/ (accessed 10 October 2014).

Perls, F., Herrerline, F.R., and Goodman, P. (1951/2009) *Gestalt Therapy: Excitement and growth in the human personality.* London: Souvenir Press.

Robinson, K. (2006) 'Schools kill creativity'. Online. www.ted.com/talks/ken_robinson_says_schools_kill_ creativity.html (accessed 26 December 2009).

Rogers, C.R. (1951) *Client-Centred Therapy: Its current practice, implications and therapy.* London: Constable and Robinson.

Room 13 International (2012) 'The story of Room 13'. Online: http://room13international.org/about/the-story-of-room-13 (accessed 8 July 2014).

Schulkin, J. (2005) *Curt Richter: A life in the laboratory.* Baltimore: Johns Hopkins University Press.

Selekman, D.M. (1997) *Solution-Focused Therapy with Children: Harnessing family strengths for systemic change.* New York: Guilford Press.

Seligman, M., and Maier, S. (1967) 'Failure to escape traumatic shock'. *Journal of Experimental Psychology,* 74 (1), 1–9.

Shapiro, L. (2011) *Embodied Cognition.* London: Routledge.

Social Mobility and Child Poverty Commission (2014). *Response to the Consultation on the Child Poverty Strategy 2014 to 2017.* London: SMCP. Online. www.gov.uk/government/uploads/system/uploads/attachment_data/file/318062/2b_Poverty_Response_-_Final.pdf (accessed 10 October 2014).

Townsend, P. (1979) *Poverty in the United Kingdom: A Survey of Household Resources and Standards of Living.* Harmondsworth: Penguin.

Trussell Trust (2013) *Biggest Ever Increase in UK Foodbank Use: 170% rise in numbers turning to foodbanks in last 12 months.* Salisbury: Trussell Trust. Online. www.trusselltrust.org/resources/documents/Press/BIGGEST-EVER-INCREASE-IN-UK-FOODBANK-USE.pdf (accessed 10 October 2014).

Van Evra, J. (1990) *Television and Child Development.* Hillsdale, NJ: Lawrence Erlbaum Associates.

Wallace, Catherine M. (2001) 'Seven Don'ts Every Parent Should Do'. Online. www.catherinemwallace.com/Home/essays/seven-donts-every-parent-should-do (accessed 8 October 2014).

White, M., and Epston, D. (1990) *Narrative Means to Therapeutic Ends.* New York: W.W. Norton.

Whitham, G. (2012) *Child Poverty in 2012: It shouldn't happen here.* Manchester: Save the Children. Online. www.savethechildren.org.uk/resources/online-library/child-poverty-2012-it-shouldnt-happen-here (accessed 10 October 2014).

Wilkin, A., Gulliver, C., and Kinder, K. (2005) *Serious Play: An evaluation of arts activities in pupil referral units and learning support units.* London: Calouste Gulbenkian Foundation. Online. www.gulbenkian.org.uk/pdffiles/--item-1227-192-Serious-play.pdf (accessed 10 October 2014).

Wilsher, T. (2007) *The Mask Handbook: A Practical Guide.* London: Routledge.

Winnicott, D. (1971) *Playing and Reality*. London: Tavistock.

Zimmerman, M. (1990) 'Toward a theory of learned hopefulness: A structural model analysis of participation and empowerment'. *Journal of Research in Personality*, 24, 71–86.

Index